Fall 2006   Vol. XXVI, no. 3
ISSN: 0276-0045   ISBN-13: 1-56478-464-3   ISBN-10: 1-56478-464-9

THE REVIEW OF CONTEMPORARY FICTION

Editor

JOHN O'BRIEN
Illinois State University

Managing Editor

E. J. VAN LANEN

Guest Editors

MARY G. BERG
PAMELA CARMELL
ANNE FOUNTAIN

Associate Editor

IRVING MALIN

Book Review Editor

JEREMY M. DAVIES

Production & Design

N. J. FURL

www.dalkeyarchive.com

The *Review of Contemporary Fiction* is published three times each year
(January, June, September).
ISSN 0276-0045.
Subscription prices are as follows:

Single volume (three issues):
Individuals: $17.00; foreign, add $3.50.
Institutions: $26.00; foreign, add $3.50.

This issue is partially supported by a grant from
the Illinois Arts Council, a state agency.

Indexed in *American Humanities Index, International Bibliography of
Periodical Literature, International Bibliography of Book
Reviews, MLA Bibliography*, and *Book Review Index*. Abstracted
in *Abstracts of English Studies*.

The *Review of Contemporary Fiction* is also available on 16mm
microfilm, 35mm microfilm, and 105mm microfiche from
University Microfilms International, 300 North Zeeb Road,
Ann Arbor, MI 48106-1346.

www.dalkeyarchive.com

THE REVIEW OF CONTEMPORARY FICTION

BACK ISSUES AVAILABLE

Back issues are still available for the following numbers of the
Review of Contemporary Fiction ($8 each unless otherwise noted):

Individuals receive a 10% discount on orders of one issue and a 20% discount on orders
of two or more issues. To place an order, use the form on the last page of this issue.

Contents

Guest Editors' Note

New Cuban Fiction presents recent short stories by fifteen of the best writers on the island. These fifteen very different authors, translated here by eight translators in order to better retain the remarkable diversity of voices, write primarily about current times and the challenges of survival since the collapse of the Soviet Union, when the Cuban economy slipped into the so-called "Special Period" of 1990s scarcities and ingenious coping strategies.

Fifteen different perspectives on Cuban realities are presented here, all sharp-eyed perceptions of flaws and merits, limitations and freedoms, and the tensions of living (and defining) Cubanness on this island of eleven million people, ninety miles from the Florida coast, embargoed by the U.S. for most of the past half-century yet bombarded with images of U.S. consumer culture.

These stories reflect both light and dark responses to changing times. Some are songs of despair and surrender, while others show ways to circumvent shortages and adapt to changing circumstances. Some stories are set in Havana, while others depict rural or small town Cuba. The volume includes both men and women authors, features pieces of both action and description, and presents everyday detail along with abstract concepts. Some tales are leavened by humor; many are not. Some voices make reference to the past, while some suggest the future. Awareness of the present informs all of these fictions, and many address controversial topics: homosexuality, prostitution, drugs, crime, exile, disillusionment, skepticism. But the predominant tone is of celebration and survival, one of rejoicing at the warmth and strength of human commitments, and at the complex variety of Cuban experiences.

The wide variety of writing styles included in *New Cuban Fiction* offers testimony to the vibrancy of current Cuban fiction. At the same time, the mention of literary icons such as Julio Cortázar, Alfonsina Storni and Alejo Carpentier and others remind us of the connection these works have with the wider world of Latin American writing. Most importantly, this anthology brings stories by many of the best current Cuban writers to English-speaking readers, and provides at least glimpses of Cuba in 2006, an island on the edge of change and challenge.

—*Mary G. Berg, Pamela Carmell, and Anne Fountain*

Lost Places

Antonio José Ponte

(Obispo Street, Old Havana)

This is my street. Obispo belongs to me, if a person can own a street without having a business or a house on it, or even the house of a lover or a friend on it. I discovered an old photograph of it in an encyclopedia from the beginning of the century: the street of shops, with striped awnings lining the two sidewalks, looks like a *souk*, an Arabian bazaar, seen from above. Some time ago I wrote that the street in some ways resembled a beach. Bookstores line its upper end and at the lower end the street opens onto the plaza and the port. At that time one of the bookstores sold Russian books and Soviet ships passed through the port. Obispo was contained between those two labels in cyrillic: the title of a book and the name of a ship.

Now its nature has changed a great deal. I no longer see it as a beach, but as a dry riverbed, a river of the eighties. With time even the geography of a street turns grim. Obispo is the bed of an extinct river. The water has gone and left two immense bluffs, two rows of façades.

(Paseo del Prado: empathy with a tree)

It is the first tree that faces the sea. Prado, particularly in winter, seems to me like a ship headed toward the water.

The tree must be a laurel, if the other trees of the Paseo are laurels. A laurel twisted by the wind.

When the northerlies arrive, they go along Prado, and the laurel bends before the gusts like a bony courtesan, a humpback.

At a certain time of the year, during a false autumn, the Indian almonds of the Avenida del Puerto take on fabulous beauty: greens and reds filter light just as stained glass does, and flesh seen beneath the leaves takes on splendorous colors . . . In Parque Central some nameless trees blossom in yellow chains, the air passing through them ignites and we are inside a colored photograph . . . But the first laurel of Prado, humpbacked and all, is my tree in the city. Something not yet a symbol, something confusing, never clarified, draws me to it often.

Pointing to a Greek dog, Empedocles was asked, "What makes that dog come and always sit on the same tile?"

"Empathy," Empedocles answered, "there's empathy between the dog and the tile."

(Teahouse of Mercaderes, Old Havana)

I wrote a novel there in the teahouse on Mercaderes Street. That is, the novel had pages that happened there and I would have liked to write the whole book at one of its tables, the way Europeans write in a café. However, the waitresses wouldn't let anyone write there. They were very strict about it. They would count twenty minutes or so, bring the check and put us out. They didn't trust us, us writers.

I had conversations there with many people: now gone, dead, forgotten. I learned to converse at those tables. I went there every day. When I remember the eighties, I remember myself there.

(A park in Vedado)

And then said it was decided, it was all over. What could I say to that? I looked at our surroundings, I was looking with the resignation and shock of a person who is going to die as soon as day breaks.

"All right," I said, "better that we not go back together."

I don't know how long I stayed in that park alone. I looked at details impossible to forget even now.

A year earlier a city had appeared where nothing had been before. First a window lit up and after that everything began to grow. Because the window belonged to a building, the building to a suddenly animated street, the street to a neighborhood, and the neighborhood to a city that emerged from that window.

And now it would disappear, Atlantis or Carthage or Guernica or Pompeii.

(In the old quarter of the whores)

They must be drying their hair in the sun
the whores of back then who are still alive.
Around their necks a damp towel,
some petals in a pail of water,
their heads of vanquished queens watching a sparrow.

The sparrow is looking for rice grains scattered on the ground.
What bird's fantasy would not hold the memory
that would save one grain and one night and one man
from so many men and nights that were.

With yellow nails like bird claws the women
lift strands so the sun will reach the skull.
How sad at this hour are the whores of back then
as they prepare their rice and fry an egg and sweet plantain in oil.

In the old quarter of the whores weariness overwhelms.
What so many books, so many family pictures try to awaken,
something nameable with density, depth, the essence of human life,
is found here.
Weariness at seeing photos of groups of heads:
celebrations, rites, convictions, crowds, packed train cars.
In the quarter of repeated gestures
the air has as many layers as puff pastry.
The superpositions, the heaping up
of one generation over earlier ones,
the humus of men weighs down.
In this place one can speak of the denseness of the past as in no other.

Translation by Cola Franzen

Only Afternoon in Granada

Antonio José Ponte

I lived just one afternoon in Granada. I climbed up to the Arab quarter. Think of a labyrinth spread over a hillside.

I went into a tea house, a *tetería*. The house had wooden walls and was built as a series of cubicles, labyrinth within a labyrinth, with low ceilings and tables. The air was thick and the music Arabic. It seemed to me that this song, unlike others, did not advance in time.

I sat down on leather cushions with gilded designs. The small flame of an oil lamp was burning on the table. It was neither hot nor cold inside although outside it was winter.

One of the proprietors (the owners were two brothers) handed me a menu. The way he was dressed reminded me of Isak Dinesen's Somalian servant in Africa. The menu was enormous; I ordered mango tea. I thought about Dinesen and about Paul Bowles. I said to myself: either this is a dream or I am in Tangiers. (My paternal grandmother is peeling a mandarine and asks if I wish a tangerine.)

The utensils they brought with the tea were made of clay and I noticed the sieve was of clay also. Later I went out into the street and back down the hill. I asked what the name of that district of the city was.

They answered with an Arabic word that began with al-, like alfalfa or alcove.

The next afternoon I had already forgotten the name. No matter how hard I searched, I couldn't remember it. One night, when I'd forgotten about searching, I got on a bus. A bus in Havana. It was one that had come from Spain; some group in Andalusia had donated it. It immediately seemed very familiar to me. The route indicated by the sign was a route in Spain. I looked at a small map over the window. It had colored lines giving the names of La Alhambra and Generalife. Albaicín was what that district was called where I lived one afternoon.

The bus was traveling through a dark Havana. I could imagine myself once again in Granada.

In *À rebours*, the novel by Huysmans, his protagonist in Paris decides to visit London. He prepares for the trip, and with plenty of time before taking the boat, goes into an English restaurant and orders English dishes. His meal finished, he asks his coachman to take him home, because he's already been in London. Lately I've taken Dutch, Swedish or German buses without ever moving from here. They keep their original signs but run along Havana streets. They happily undermine all directions, make Havana even more of a fable.

Translation by Cola Franzen

My Mother the Writer

Adelaida Fernández de Juan

Today I went out with my mother.

One of her friends wrote a book and besides giving a lot of lunches and a few dinners in his honor, and listening to him (my mother, not me), today we went to the place where they presented the book. At the presentation were other friends of my mother, friends of the author of the book, and other writers. All of the friends were writers. There were only a few women there and no children besides me. The women were more or less my mother's age, and they looked alike. They looked like each other and like my mother—overall, they were a group of pretty similar-looking women. All of them, like my mother, wore those loose dresses that go from the neck to the feet, without anyone being able to guess anything about the tits or butts of these women who get together every once in a while.

It's not unusual for them to come to our house. When they come—together or separately, I don't care, I already told you what their dresses are like, as if they didn't have tits or anything worthwhile—my mother makes tea and they start saying bad things about the writers that are men.

It's not just my mother who talks. They all say things that I only half understand, but I know they are bad, really bad. After all of them say how much I look like "that sonofabitch who left the island" when my mom makes me greet them, I shut myself in my room. First I jack off trying to imagine their tits, and later, while I do my homework, I listen to the conversations coming from the living room where they're gathered.

"They don't have us in mind" . . . "those bastards who get to travel" . . . "they're all in that same group" . . . "they gave him the prize because he's a man" are some examples.

When I say I half understand, it's so that I won't seem stupid. Actually, I don't understand any of it. If "that sonofabitch" left, why do my mom and the others want to travel? What is this about a famous group anyway? What could being male or female have to do with a prize?

I always win the history and math competitions at school, and no one has ever told me that I win because I'm male. According to my mother, I am the smartest child who's ever been born and that's why I always win. She also says that being born male is a passport for life. I have no idea what that means, but I know it's good, really good.

After drinking tea and saying bad things about the men who are writers, the women talk about really boring things that no one is interested in, like lettuce soaps, aloe creams, cucumber lotions and other disgusting stuff like that. That's when I regret having jacked off thinking about one of them, but it's too late.

Anyway, if the men writers visit us (I like using the plural, as if they came to see me) they don't drink tea but instead rum, which they bring themselves.

I also have to greet them in the living room and hear that I look like "that sonofabitch." Some of the men don't say the last part, ". . . that left"; they just say "that sonofabitch," but it's basically the same. They always tell me how I've grown, that I should take care of my mother, that she is the most beautiful writer in Cuba, and that I should drink rum with them. Clearly I say YES to the first sentences and NO to the last one without even having to look at my mom. On days like that, all my mother's royal qualities come out, and I could imagine her as a queen.

Surrounded by them, she smiles like I think the queen bee would with the drones. I don't dare to look at her much. I'm wondering if they're from the famous group that gives prizes only to others from within its circle.

It's not good to listen in on conversations, and rum isn't good either. They drink it without knowing that later my mom calls them a "bunch of drunks" when they leave, which isn't good either, but she doesn't know I hear everything.

We are always keeping a close eye (and this time the plural is serious) on the results of the contests. If it were up to me, she would win all of them. I can't think of another house in the world that depends as much on prizes as we do. My skates, for example, took my mother more than six months. It was a book called *Defended Woman*. The wicker set we have in the living room (where the writer friends come sit together) came from a novel that my mother called *Sexuality and Independence* (I should say that all her titles are complicated).

With my backpack for school we weren't so lucky. We were going to buy it with a prize my mother was going to win in a magazine. This was going to happen in August, in time for the beginning of school. A man (I assume from the famous group) won first prize. That's why my backpack isn't so good: because it's an honorable mention backpack.

Things like chickens and cleaning mops don't worry my mother and me. We can get by on the provincial prizes. It doesn't matter if the contest is about love, or owls, or the Republic.

My mother writes for her daily bread and butter (that's what she says).

These are things that I respect a lot.

When it gets near my birthday, my mom writes like crazy, day and night. My cargo pants and my shirt with the alligator on it came from a book of stories. It's called *Looking for a Lover*, and my mother made me swear I'd never read it. According to her it's a piece of shit, but the truth is, the clothes are great.

Sometimes the other women who write win, and they all get together to celebrate. I don't understand how my mother can be happy about that. I also don't understand how she stands being friends with the person who could deprive us, for example, of the lamp we need in my room. We have a list of the things we need, my mother and I. She writes the complicated title of the possible book next to each one.

The Sun that Doesn't Sleep was beside the Washing Machine, *The Way We Were Then* is by the Kitchen Table. Next to my Lamp is *Feminine Revindication*.

I say "is" because it's still there. That's the book we just lost with. We already got the washing machine and the table, but my lamp is still on the list. The man we went to congratulate won.

After hearing about how marvelous the winner is, how good the book is and all that, my mother hugged the two writers. First the one who talked (if he said what he said it's because he belongs to their group, I imagine) and then the one who won (he'll probably be even more famous than the group now).

I don't know why I went out with my mom today. To top it all off, I couldn't even see a single tit that was worth the trouble.

Translation by Mary G. Berg

My Love and My Sugarcane

José Antonio Quintana Veiga

He came by again to talk about the land. He's not quite so elegant now. The same clothes, I mean, but all ten years older—the guayabera shirts, the cowboy pants, the riding boots, and Him. The guayaberas are faded and you can see through them, though they're not mended anywhere because his wife is an artist when it comes to washing fine clothes. He doesn't shave every day, or smell any longer of Bebito cologne. He came by on his older daughter's bike, with That Look deep down in his eyes. Beautiful eyes that reflect the loyalty of his tender soul, even though he'll be turning fifty soon. Yes, because it's twenty years since He first began to take an interest in my land. I was ten when my father died, may he rest in peace, and a few months later came that mysterious pronouncement. "What you need isn't Land, but Space to fulfill all the Promise that lurks between one eyebrow and the other. You'll have enough Time." When I demanded an explanation, He always said the same thing, just as mysterious. "When you can explain it yourself, then it will be worthwhile for you to understand."

I never had a chance to be Naive, let alone Foolish. My land, my sixty acres planted with Cane that stands before my eyes right now, he wasn't after it. Much less these days, since he's been elected President of the UBPC,[*] which makes him lord or co-owner of almost fifty times that much. My house ought to be His House, but he lives in El Batey with all the comforts of town—next door to the ration-book store and the other one where you can shop with Bonus Coupons. The family doctor is his neighbor too—he just has to cross the yard to get his blood pressure taken, which anyway never rises or falls. His wife, the poor thing, is Messed Up with perpetual bouts of asthma. Worse now, since medicines have gotten so scarce, and if you can Acquire them, it's from the resellers who buy in Havana at one price and sell here for a hundred times more. I couldn't wish

---

[*]UBPCs (Basic Units of Cooperative Production) are the type of semi-private cooperative to which many state farms were converted in the 1990s. "He" was presumably manager of a state farm in the earlier years of the story, though in its present moment, in the '90s, he is the elected director of the UBPC. The "Bonus Coupon" store referred to in the next sentence sells goods normally sold only for hard currency, in this case to holders of coupons issued to reward high production or effort in the harvest and milling of cane.

the poor woman's death, but if she dies, let it be the Yankees' fault, not mine. He'd come to live in my house then.

His visits don't have anything to do with my money, either. Those Fabulous thousands and thousands of pesos that the gossips of El Batey say I've been hiding ever since my father died, may he rest in peace—they don't exist and never did. If Don Antonio left me Four Pesos, then I ate them up in little treats before I turned fifteen, and He understands that better than anyone. When we got into the Special Period, sure, a suckling pig started to be worth two or even three thousand pesos, and I sold my share of them, but how much did a pack of cigarettes cost? Forty! And a bottle of bad rum? Two hundred! Anyway, it was thanks to my piglets that his daughter, the owner of that bicycle, had a Decent Wedding and could enjoy her Symbolic Loss of Virginity between new sheets. You know what a new bed sheet was going for in the year 1993, don't you? A Virgin Herself! That's what Yurisleidis told me, María del Carmen's daughter, who had to Sell Her Ass to the head of the warehouse for a new sheet—because that son of a b— wouldn't take money at all. I Acquired the ones I'm talking about with money, but they cost an Arm and a Leg.

In the harvest of '94 I took a loss on my cane. They paid me seventeen-thirty per hundred arrobas, while it cost me twenty per to grow and harvest it. That includes what little fertilizer I could Acquire from the ex-president of the UBPC, who comes to me now with the story that this is why they fired him. As if Everyone didn't know that happened because he conspired with every illegal cow-slaughterer in El Batey. And he sold half the gasoline that was supplied to the UBPC! It's true that the gas assigned to cane growing wasn't enough even to light the oil lamps of the thousand and one nights of blackouts, but I agree with our Representative that Shortage Doesn't Justify Theft. The next year's harvest, '95, was worse. We private growers didn't have either a mini-tractor or a single pair of oxen among us, and we couldn't take advantage of the opportunities the UBPC had, which were more fertilizer, herbicide, and fuel than it needed. Under the table, He did help out some Private Growers, but I didn't get so much as a mouthful of gas or a teaspoon of fertilizer. He was so severe with me that even his own children and friends (including the Representative) criticized him to his face and called it extremism on his part. When the new director of the Sugar Complex asked me why my cane hadn't improved its yield this year, I told him the truth. The man got mad and sent for Him, to bawl him out. But He wasn't angry at me for complaining. When he called me Gossip and Tattletale in public, he did it with his damned Enchanting Smile, which always gives me Chills underneath my belly button. Sometimes my legs even Go Weak when that son-of-some-saint smiles at me this way.

And mark one thing—He says it's My Smile that captivates him. The day I turned fourteen he wrote me a poem about my smile that gave me my First Orgasm, the very first. I'll write it down here so you can see for yourselves:

BERTICA

She's barely there
in terms of flesh and bone
until she smiles—
that quality smile!
that multiplies its surroundings
into Biblical images
brought to life by miraculous flashes
of Caribbean heresy.
Then she mounts to the pulpit
with her robe rolled high
and breaks out with a swear-word
and covers any bet
as to whether or not happiness
can be built with her smile alone.

I felt so praised. Imagine! A girl like me: very young then, a country girl, brought up by a man who was too rough and too ready with the whip. Imagine how sensitive such a girl is to the influence of words like those. Simple, I admit, but so full of flattery. Of course, I showed the little poem to Everyone: my girlfriends in Junior High, my teachers, the Representative. All of them, without exception, told me that it seemed more like a Documentary about me than a poem, because that's exactly how I was, the swear-words too. From then on, He was considered a Poet by everyone except his wife, who thought he was Something Else. I showed her the Poem, which wasn't so innocent a thing to do as you're thinking, and she looked at me over her glasses—I remember she was mending some blue socks—and said, "The poetry is pretty, and you deserve it, but If You Fuck My Husband, I'm going to Burn Your House Down." I've never spoken to her since.

So, it's not my money that brings him around here, because I still owe money to the bank. Maybe next year I'll be better off. My cane is doing well, and the yield ought to double, because I planted fifteen acres in the winter, rehabilitated another thirty, and left the other fifteen alone, meaning I didn't cut them this year, and they're looking quite fine. The rain has been Very Opportune, the fertilizer showed up Just in Time, and I didn't give the weeds a chance to seed. I think I'm going to have a good harvest, though not as good as in my father's best years, when he managed to get three hundred thousand arrobas out of this little patch of ground. Last year He brought me a new seed variety—it's called Cuba 1051—which they gave him in Havana to try out in the UBPC. That's what I planted in the winter. Every time He comes by, he talks about that new cane. He's in love with it. He's even claimed that Cuba 1051 is the cane that's going to pull the country out of the Special Period. That's an exaggeration, of course, but I know how he feels. This variety is good, maybe even exceptional, so let's wait and see.

Anyway, don't go thinking that his interest in my cane is all that brings him around. He can go up and down my Fields without asking anyone's permission. And I'm all for it, because his Eye for pests and diseases beats any grower's around here, and he clues me in. Like the mice—an infestation of mice broke out in a little field I've got by the highway, and if not for Him, they would have ruined all the cane. That's the field I use for seed, where I've got the best varieties to come out of the Research Station. It's like a Seed Bank, and I watch to see How They Behave, to choose the ones to plant more widely. Believe me, this Man isn't satisfied to walk his three thousand acres. He's got to walk the neighboring fields, mine included, as well. That's how he spotted the mouse attack and I was able to save my Seed Bank. No farmer around here takes offense when He decides to check out their fields. And he doesn't do it in a stuck-up way, with any air of superiority. He comes to you and says, "I had to cross your property because I was In a Hurry, and so By Accident I saw that that little field is full of whip fungus. Better go take a look." And thanks to his "hurry" and his "accidents," many folks around here have had time to save their cane from some misfortune which was about to occur. Of course, he doesn't mention that his checking out the neighboring fields protects the fields of the UBPC, but that's the case.

That precaution isn't new. I remember when I'd just graduated from high school, in fact it was the day I turned sixteen, he appeared at my uncle's house—my father's older brother, may he rest in peace—and gave us all a speech about How to Protect the Jaronú 60-5 so it didn't turn susceptible to fungus. That's an exceptional variety, very productive and resistant to almost all diseases, besides growing well in any kind of ground. All the growers around here fell in love with it, and in four or five years they planted so much that it took up almost sixty per cent of the area sown in cane. "That's dangerous," He said to us, still on his feet and with his hat in his hand. Then he grabbed a stool and leaned it back against the post that supports the roof of the kitchen, since the kitchen was where they entertained guests in my uncle's house. We all waited, me with my mouth open, because I loved the timbre of his voice and all that he knew about cane. With his eyes lit up by a Passion like a Revelation, avoiding mine which were eating him up with a more Earthly

Passion, he explained that a variety like the Jaronú 60-5 had to be protected. The first thing was to avoid extending it more than the specialists recommended: twenty five percent of the area, at the most. He said that there were other varieties which were Also good, which the rest of the area could be planted with. As an example, he pointed to one of the districts of the Sugar Complex that He administered directly, and invited us all to come by there the Next Sunday so we could see it *in situ* (he's always liked those Latin phrases, by the way). We'd see how he'd distributed the varieties so that the Jaronú would yield All That It Could Give without deteriorating from excess use.

I went to that Demonstration as decked out as could be. When he saw me, he took me by the arm and led me away from the group of relatives and friends. "What are you doing here?" he said. "Shouldn't you be in Havana starting Medical School? Wasn't that what you promised your father you were going to do? And why are you dressed up for a night out, to come here and look at cane?" I couldn't help being impressed by his deep voice and friendly tone, and I explained I didn't want to be a Doctor any more, but an Agronomic Engineer, and there was no point arguing about it because I'd already registered at the university for that. As for my outfit, I was Dressed Like That because I wanted to Impress Him, so he'd come with me when the tour of the cane was done, to swim in the river and eat mangoes, I hoped. I said all that with plenty of fawning and flattery, but I looked him straight in the eye. That did the trick. Whenever I talk to him as equal to equal, it sweeps his defenses away. He didn't give me any more trouble, and returned to His Affairs with Madame Cane. That was the day I realized he was making sure none of us did anything stupid with our cane so as to protect the land under his responsibility, which in those days belonged to the state. He does the same now in the UBPC. After a while, he got the population of Jaronú 60-5 down to about 35 percent. More than that even He couldn't do.

The issue of my studies was discussed a lot within my family. I mean my living uncles and my cousins, because all the rest are dead. It's not that my relatives die young, it's that when I was born my father was Already Sixty and my mother Twenty-Five. Papa died at seventy from being kicked by a cow. My mother had left for Havana before I turned three, and then, in '80, she hooked up with some Kid from Around There and they took off for the United States through Mariel. All this I've been told, because I don't even remember her. So my change of career was an excuse to go live Permanently in the house my father left me, a big old wooden one with a zinc roof, later fixed up and extended after His wife tried to burn it down. Well, in fact she did burn it—she put it to the torch on All Four Sides—but the repair work was excellent and didn't leave any reminders of the fire. When she threatened to Burn it Again, I took the necessary precautions: I rebuilt it with concrete blocks, gave it a cement roof thirty centimeters thick, and I put four fifty-gallon water tanks on top. To burn it down now, you'd have to drop napalm on it. I've lived here with some of my cousins and their husbands for twelve years. That was the alternative my uncles gave me, if I wasn't going to satisfy their desires to have a Doctor Niece.

In truth I did have a vocation for medicine, but I was afraid that after I graduated they'd send me to work in the city and take me away from Him, so I decided to be an Agronomist and specialize in Cane. He felt very flattered by my decision, although he's never told me that right out. The Representative also took my side, when the Party Members of the Sugar Complex, in that year's annual meeting, tried to meddle in my affairs. They were put up to it by one of my uncles, who was the First Secretary of the Party in the town. Claiming I was an orphan and the Smartest Girl in the area, they declared themselves the Guarantors of my Future. I was told that in the meeting the Representative got Very Angry and said the Party couldn't meddle in this for the simple reason that they Had No Right. One of the meddlers replied that they weren't trying to Impose a Career, but to discuss with me and Make Me Think about the usefulness of my becoming a Doctor because there were more Agronomists than were needed. Then the Representative looked at Him, who'd kept very quiet, as if asking for help. He stood up very slowly, they say, walked to the blackboard at the back of the room, and gave an Illustrated Lecture on the future of Agriculture in general, Sugar Cane in particular, and the real needs for Highly Qualified Experts in the next five or ten years. His speech provided a lot of grist for the mill in El Batey and for miles around. The version I heard made me so happy, it was like Coitus in the middle of the day. It went more or less like this: "Bertica is not only the Most Intelligent Woman produced by our town and twenty kilometers on every side, but also the most beautiful, pretty, daring, honorable, and frank that I've known since the Day I was Born. If she becomes a doctor, with such qualities, I doubt she'll be allowed to return to this corner of Cuba, and probably not to this province at all. As an Agronomist she also runs this risk, but less severely, taking into account that She, for some very powerful reason, Loves this place and is determined to return. Havana may need Exceptional Doctors, but Agronomists with those characteristics are needed here, and no one's going to try to take her away from us. My humble opinion is that She made the right decision of her own free will, which is How It Ought To Be."

They say that when he finished, The Silence was so thick that when the First Secretary of the Party Committee knocked his fist on the table to announce the end of the discussion, everybody jumped from fright. Of course, as always happened in those meetings, all of El Batey knew what had been discussed and decided even before the assembly was adjourned, and knew who had been on which side. One time a few years ago, this bothered the leaders so much that they ordered an Investigation because a certain very sensitive and secret Issue had leaked out. It seemed that in an argument between two women in the bodega one said to the other that her husband had been sanctioned in the Party because she'd Cheated on Him and he'd let it Go By. When she said this, the Secretary of the nucleus in the Mill happened to be standing there, and he raised a hue and cry so the Investigation was begun. They asked that first woman who had given her The Information and she said without hesitation, "It was So and So." When they asked So and So, she confessed it was Such and Such. And so on, each to the next, until they'd put together a chain of twenty-four people and reached the conclusion that The Whole Town knew—without finding out who the informant was, of course. The measure they took to counteract this kind of leak was to warn the members that everyone who didn't want Their Shit known all around town better just Keep Themselves Clean. Now the Party assemblies aren't secret any more, so if anyone asks, you can tell down to the last detail what was said and what was not.

Well, so that one where they discussed my decision to study Agronomy instead of Medicine, it was secret, but I heard all about it right away. When He came to my house to explain how my cane should be cut in the harvest that was about to start, I thanked him for his praise and told him, with absolute sincerity, that I considered it underserved. That day was unforgettable for me, doubly so, because besides teaching me how to care for the root structure when harvesting my fields, he wrote his second poem, also dedicated to me, sitting at my kitchen table. I'll show it to you, to see what you think.

BERTICA (II)

You'll never be a memory
filed away in my past
not the loose end of a story
nor one explained at last.

You'll never be the breeze
evanescent and mild
nor the full moon in eclipse
nor the shadow of a smile

You won't be a flower's petal
that perishes at a chill
nor the drama that moves us
nor a nightingale's trill

You'll just be the essence
of all that's alive
the marrow that nourishes
the factor that decides

Poetry's true sex
and God's only love
the place they come together
the orgasm of life.

Imagine that! I was just a kid, really, even though I was in college and taking care of my house and my cane. So I cried. Oh Lord how I cried that day! How beautifully! That Fabulous Man in front of me, in my kitchen, in my house, telling me those things. I read the poem two or three times without saying a word because my tears were choking me. He asked me to make him some coffee and I put the pot on the stove without even filling it. I was shaking for more than an hour. Even now, my eyes fill up when I remember that day. I feel like Running through every Canefield of the Sugar Complex till I find him and ask him to swear by his grandchildren that I'll forever be his Only Love.

It's not my cane that brings him around here so often, but his Passion for the cane is strong. Many times I've felt, and even resigned myself to accept it, that His Love for Me is a by-product of His Love for the Cane. At first it was just a sensation, an inkling, that became a certainty when I graduated with my engineering degree and was sent to do my social service stint in the provincial Agricultural Research Station, the EPICA as everyone says. Really, I don't have a researcher's soul, and the most convincing proof is that only two men have seen me naked: my papa and Him. If the man I have seems Supreme to me, compared with what other women are Said to Have, then what would be the point of risking it in search of something the same or worse? Still I had to accept my post in the EPICA and find a way to link my solid Sense of Reality when it comes to sugar cane with the Imaginative and Meticulous tendency of the researchers. Luckily, research also needs people who know how to do things in the traditional way. They assigned me to work in the area of Genetics, whose main goal is to develop better varieties, but the process (twelve to fifteen years) seems excessively long to me. So as not to suffer, I said to myself, "Bertica, your task is to make sure that all this cane sown around here gets taken care of the way God Desires, and produces Lots of Sugar as a result. Let the Geneticists worry about Which is Which."

Of course, I'm putting the cart before the horse, because the truth is that at first I flatly refused to work with the Researchers, for fear of getting caught up in their vice of over-specialization. But finally I had to argue it out with Him. I was staying home, determined to take care of my cane and pay the state back every last cent of what my education had cost, when the director of the EPICA, learning of my Insolence (the rector of the university told him I was Spoiled), visited me and spoke eloquently of the beauties and attractions of Research. He promised me the moon and the stars including Specialist Courses abroad. Which is to say, he tried to conquer me with counterproductive arguments. What's worse, I compared him to my Ideal, and I didn't see that Extraordinary Love for Cane that comes out of my Loved One's pores even when he sleeps. I listened with exquisite courtesy and said goodbye with my best smile, but I confirmed my decision to stay home. The director wouldn't give up, so he went to see Him, to complain about my "irrational attitude" and ask him to intervene, taking into account the Respect and the Consideration he was accorded on all sides. Before nightfall, He knocked on my door, wearing his handsomest guayabera and some Camaguey boots that I had given him the previous Valentine's Day. I was in the kitchen, working on dinner, and suddenly realized it was Him and what he had come about. I was still trying to get my hair in place when I bumped up against His Smile. My God, the smile of that Man, as Carilda says, it throws me for a loop. I forgot everything I'd planned to say to him. As usual, we started off talking about my cane and the neighbors'. Then he asked me, as if by accident, when I was supposed to report to work at the EPICA. "Last week," I told him, and put my guard up. He lowered his head, as if this bothered him a lot, and said, "Damn, what we really need is someone from around here to work for a while with those people at the EPICA. Whatever they seem like, they do know A Lot about Cane and they're very up to date about what's going in on The World in that sense. But it has to be somebody who can absorb everything within two or three years. Not some dummy who'll waste everyone's time." He looked at me sadly and added, "I know you don't want to go, but if we don't find somebody, then—if they'll let me—I'll have to do it myself."

Go figure! My eyes teared right up. He was sitting down and I was standing but I knelt down beside him and took his hands, always so warm. "Do you want me to go?" I asked him. He answered with another question. "Will it hurt you?" And he added right away: "I don't want you to do anything that will hurt you." Then I cried a little, because I like to cry when I have Such Beautiful Moments in my life, so later I can recall them and cry again. He gave me a little kiss in the forehead and asked me not to cry, because he'd find some other solution. Right away I told him no, I'd Go, because anything I could do for Him made me Happy, and in the EPICA I'd be Very Happy after all. He told me to promise—to promise him I'd be Happy—and I did. We sealed the agreement with an Unforgettable Kiss like in the movies. That night I slept in peace and satisfied I was his Only Love, after the cane. I vowed to learn so much about cane that He'd have no other choice but to love me at least as much.

Since my high school days, many people—teachers, friends, relatives, and suitors—have told me that my Lovesick Love for a man twenty years older, and married, stemmed from the Isolation in which I lived. I was a victim of Geographic Fatalism, in short. They predicted a gradual disappointment when I matured as a Woman and came to know New Worlds and the new men who lived in them. Here in El Batey, they all said, He doesn't have any competition. He's got this Aura of The Indispensable Man created by his extraordinary knowledge about the cultivation of Sugar Cane and many other subjects related to that. The fact is, few of them recognize his Exceptional Humanity, or worse still, they consider him irresponsible or unscrupulous, for maintaining Dubious Relations with a young girl, an orphan, with no relatives Man Enough to defend her from him. In parentheses, let me say that my two younger uncles and three of their sons, my cousins, fought in the war in Angola and won medals For Bravery, and if they never messed with Him, it was simply because he was Their Commander in the war and they respected him like a god. Once, when someone tried to incite them to call him to account for his relations with me, my uncle answered with words that I retain with much Love in my memory and heart. My uncle said, "That man isn't afraid of bullets, bombs, mines, hunger, cold, snakes, diseases, death, or his commanders. What am I going to threaten him with?" So, accusing my relatives of lack of Manhood was an outrage. Personally I wasn't worried that the pressure of Public Opinion would take him away from me. We talked about this on the day when, after repeated invitations on my part, He accepted being The Love of My Life, on one Condition, which was: I had to become, by applying myself to my studies and by my social and private conduct, an Exceptional Woman. He explained that only this would justify a Man of his age and social responsibility, married and with children, having such relations with a Snotnose like me. He added that if, on the contrary, I didn't turn out to be Quite a Woman, then Ipso Facto the whole thing would end. I wasn't offended. On the contrary! I liked his frankness very much and accepted the Condition in my most passionate spirit of struggle and self-improvement.

Finally, when I confessed fear about pressures from other people, he told me not to worry, that He would assume the consequences, whatever they might be. In no case would he leave me unprotected or Alone With the Enemy.

So, like I told you, the future of My Love for Him was threatened with death by Geographic Fatalism. Once I'd gone out in the World a little farther than the limits of my farm and those of my neighbors, all that Fabulous Love would succumb to death by simple comparison. I spent five years in the university, met hundreds of young people of all Sizes, Shapes, and Colors, and the more people I got to know well, the more I held tight to Him. Then came my work in the EPICA, where I met many intelligent and interesting people, and since such research stations exist in all the provinces, I traveled throughout the Country for events related to my work and met many more people that way. One day, after a meeting in the EPICA of Palma Soriano, when we were on our way back to the city (where those of us from other provinces were staying) we stopped for a while on the bridge over the Cauto River to watch its impressive flow. I understood then that I was a Very Fortunate Woman for having been born in an anonymous little place, without rivers like the Cauto, or mountains like the Sierra Maestra, or valleys like Viñales, but with a Man Like Him. It's true that there was just one, but that one was Mine. Such reflection led me to fully understand his enigmatic phrase, that what I need isn't Land, but Space to share all this Love that I'm overflowing with. He meant space without economic or emotional limits; an Intelligent and Sensitive Space, with qualities ranging from the Intimate Heat of bed to the Immeasurability of the universe; a Human space with a Light that illuminates me from within. And I have more than enough time to explore All of it, to enjoy it in all its Purity until its Last Breath, which I'll convert into My Essence, into the Immortal Particle that All of us carry within.

I feel I'm not being honest, because I'm Skipping Over the most difficult moments, the periods of doubt, both mine and his. His Love for the cane never slipped, not even in the worst moments of the Special Period, when there wasn't enough fuel, when there were shortages of tires and parts for the machines, of fertilizer, of chemicals to combat pests and weeds, of clothes and shoes for the canecutters and even of Food. Everyone doubted the cane would survive in such circumstances, but He sought alternative solutions to save her. He was like the Right Hand of God. He summoned oxen to replace the tractors. He gathered all the leaves and chaff he could, from our Mill and the neighboring ones, to make the lack of fertilizer less of a blow. He took a chance for the first time on a Variety that he didn't like, Cuba 323, which he considered too rough for the quality of Our Soil. He planted it with the novel method of Minimum Soil Preparation and with Straw Mulch to save the work of weeding and preserve the humidity of the ground. In sum, His Love for La Caña grew strong when She most needed it, but Apparently the same Did Not Happen with me. I've read a lot about adolescence and even have participated, here in El Batey and at the university, in conferences on the subject directed by specialists, and frankly I've arrived at the conclusion that, for better or for worse, I skipped that particular stage. Adolescents tend to be rebellious, and I was not, maybe because I didn't have anyone with whom to be that way. My uncles didn't care whether I spent three days singing or three days crying, or whether I planned to be the best student in my junior high or to drop out. They treated me like a little animal that has to be fed and cared for until it can take care of itself. That's all. That's how things were until He appeared in my life. Well, He'd been in my life since papa died; I mean to say until I decided to have a Man like Him for myself alone—and if it could be him Himself, all the better. I made my Decision a little after I turned thirteen. From then on, everything I thought or did was to the end of achieving that Goal. My conduct stabilized and I behaved like the most judicious of Adult Women. At fourteen and a half I achieved the Goal, but He imposed the condition that I had to be No Ordinary Girl, and I wasn't—and wouldn't be. Still, when I turned sixteen, something happened that shook me a lot. I was never careless about my appearance, and my relations with peers, both girls and boys, were always very good. My loquacity and my love of dancing helped me a lot. But until past fifteen-and-a-half my physical development was extremely slow and put me at a Disadvantage with respect to the other girls of my age. If I didn't get to the point of developing a complex, it was because my only Feminine Attribute, my smile, continued to be a captivating one—as He told me in his first poem, you will recall. That, and because everyone knew that in spite of my Insignificant Attractions as a female, I was the Lover of a man who was more Man than most. Even the teachers treated me with a certain deference. I shared my joy with everyone, but I didn't show off. At dances I tried to pass unnoticed, just the opposite of the girls who enjoyed showing off their new pointy breasts and their quivering behinds. Then, in a flash, Spring came to me. Generously, making me grow in Optimal Proportions everywhere. After that I threw caution to the wind. It was my period of vanity, although I showed off, above all, so that he could accurately judge My New Charms. Since I was a good dancer, they invited me to all the dances, to which I mostly went alone. That is, without Him. In those days I considered jealousy to be one of the most Genuine Displays of Love, so I started to provoke situations that would make him scold me and demand that I stop being so bold. For instance, I sewed myself the most daring blouses just in the hope the He would forbid me to wear them, as happened with my girlfriends and their boyfriends sometimes. Can you imagine how disappointing it was to have a boyfriend, or a lover in my case, who never prohibited you from doing anything at all? The most I could get out of him was a few words that, more than a reproof, seemed to me a philosophical reflection. He said, "Women anxious to show off their physical charms tend not to have any other kind."

It annoyed me so much that he didn't get annoyed with me, that one day, a Saturday afternoon, I cooked up an Arrogant Provocation designed to infuriate him. I borrowed a dress from one of my girlfriends—a dress made out of one of those filmy fabrics, cut in a way that was Very Daring for that place and time. One of those dresses that, when you wear it on the street, sometimes you feel you're dressed and sometimes you feel naked instead. I showed up in the mill, in one of the workshops where he was meeting with the machine maintenance crew, who they say (and I can confirm) are the rudest of all. When I arrived, the meeting had just ended and they were offering a toast, after which there would be food, beer, and music. The men invited me to stay, and I asked him what he thought. He arranged a lock of hair on my forehead and said, "OK, but don't stay too late, because it's going to get cold and you're Not Wearing Much." Then he turned around and left. I stayed at the party out of pure pride, when what I really wanted to do was go home and cry. I didn't stay long. I drank a beer and danced two or three numbers with my cousins. When I got home—I was still living with my uncles then—I found him sleeping in my bed with his clothes on and without having taken a bath. My uncle said He'd fallen asleep talking, and together they'd managed to get him into bed. One of my cousin's husbands told me He'd spent the whole night before writing a report, and that he must be exhausted because the meeting, which started at eight in the morning, had been Very Hot. I sat down ashamed of my conduct and then lay down by his side without waking him up. I cried a little to relax and fell asleep. The next morning, when I opened my eyes, he was gone. On the night table I found a little paper, kind of greasy, which I expected to be a farewell note. It was a Poem. In fact, this was really his second poem dedicated to me, which I try to forget because I didn't like it. Maybe you'll think it's more deserving of being called a Poem than the others, but I can't judge that, because I'm too involved in it. I'll show it to you, like I did the others, to see what you think. The text is completely his. The shape it took in this final form is thanks to a Collaboration of mine.

INDEFINABLE WOMAN
(This woman may be indefinable
but I love her)

She is
This woman
is the holy spirit
of universal femininity
an avalanche of burning stars
in my dangerous madness of dreaming awake

Eyes as white as the tips of my own fingers
gaze at a whole lot of time to come
round like a genuine pleasure
like the lust of a fish
the first surprise of
her dark eyes

She is
This woman is
a feeling of homelessness
the sweet cause of all my sins
a good reason to be alive or be dead
the quality of my last waking nightmare

Feverish skin where the ends of my hair
brush along her libido born with teeth
butterfly saddled as soon as weaned
to fly in the first new moon
wings squeezed tight
against any wall

She is
This woman is
worse than indefinable
like the revenge of some god
or a tax levied on forbidden love
the erratic arrow of a drunken Cupid
bribed with the scents of virginal pubis
against the indifference of a conceited phallus
This woman is my most beautiful waking nightmare

Even at seventeen you can be aware that Indefinition is not exactly
a virtue, and that nightmares, however beautiful, are bad dreams.
Still I wasn't disappointed, because behind the Poem lay a person
who was essentially good, a Man both defined and definable who in
spite of his doubts still saw me as a Holy Spirit. I did have doubts
about His Love—or, worse, I started to feel in his indifference a
roughness that showed the lack of It. But I was afraid to venture

very far from Him—afraid of feeling helpless, because although I thought of myself as a brave woman, my bravery depended on his protection. I would have dared Anything, I mean, if and when it would have boosted my image in His Eyes. That wasn't the bravery of a free spirit, but the Blind Faith of a Woman in Love. He replaced the Father I had lost when I needed one most; he was my best friend; he was and is my Only Man in bed, my Only Love.

That Poem hurt me, but it wasn't a mortal wound. Besides, his weapon against my loose conduct was tolerance. What came next, I'd rather not confess, but I'm afraid that my story will Lose Credibility if I don't. Because of the events related to the Poem, I made up a boyfriend—to hurt him, to avenge myself for his apparent indifference. I confessed the truth two weeks later. I Made Up the plan in school with my girlfriends of my class and dorm. On weekend, when he came to pick me up at the place where the bus dropped me off, I acted Cold and didn't even return his kiss on my cheek. When he asked what was going on, I told him I had Decided to end our relationship because I had Taken Up with a teacher in school. God, what a Jerk I was. How could I underestimate a Man like Him? He never answered. Only, his eyes welled up and he started to tell me that the night before, while he was welding some farming tools, the arc had hurt his eyes so much that even his voice was affected. His Story was long and detailed, so it took up the whole way home. While he told it, sheets of tears ran down his cheeks. Then, claiming he had to go to the doctor, he left right away. That didn't give me any time to argue, although what I wanted to do was Argue a Lot, to throw his indifference and lack of love in his face and then finally, later, to tell him that the boyfriend was all a lie. I was off balance, and puzzled, and by the time I reacted it was too late. One of my cousins, when I repeated the story of His welding accident, assured me that No Accident Had Occurred. If He was crying, it was About Something Else.

I went crazy. I took off my school uniform, asked my uncle for a horse, and went searching in the cane fields all around, but nowhere did He turn up. I went to his house and called his daughter outside, but since I was so desperate and drowning in tears, the girl got scared and made me sit down and went for water. She brought me water and a diazepam too. I took it, and later I Told Her Everything. I told her I had to find him right away because I knew he was Suffering and I was afraid something bad might happen to him. Both of us cried a while, until the pill started to take effect. Since I was the one who was supposed to be More Grown Up, I calmed down and asked her to accompany me. We both climbed onto the horse and took off at random. Almost at dusk, a farmer told us he'd seen his jeep parked alongside the Central Highway, alongside the seed bank. We went there at full speed. We found him alone, measuring the height and thickness of some stalks of Cane. I jumped from the animal, ran toward Him, hugged him tight and told him I Loved Him So Much that I was going to Die For Love. Of course, I said all this through my sobs. But that was it. Nothing happened. He didn't scold me, or even stick out his tongue. He put us both in the jeep, gave the horse a tap with the whip to send it home alone, and told us, with a Wealth of Details and his Usual Passion, the history of the Cane he was measuring. From that lamentable action of mine I got something very good: a Fast Friendship with his daughter, who is my Best Friend today.

Well, so today he came again about my land. He wants us to join in the UBPC. This presumably won't affect my rights over the land very much. Really, to me personally, keeping the land doesn't matter. With my profession and the little plot I devote to growing vegetables for the family, I get enough so as not to Leave Anyone Unprotected. My two cousins who live with me are afraid I'll leave them in the Lurch if I give over the land and go live somewhere else. The fact is that I can't go anywhere. When I accepted my post as Agricultural Subdirector of the Sugar Complex, everything was crystal clear: I met my obligations to the State but continued taking care of my own Cane. Then my baby was born and things got a little more complicated. Now I'm pregnant again, with a girl, and I wouldn't Give Her Up for anything in the world. That's his main argument for why we should integrate My Cane with the UBPC's, so I can take care of the kids, at least in their earliest years. I haven't given him a categorical answer, because there isn't any hurry. The consolidation can't take place before the end of the coming harvest, '97. Meanwhile, He's taken on all the weight of his responsibility and mine. There's nothing extraordinary in that, It Was Almost Always That Way. As far as his Family Obligations, he has to Come to My House twice a day. Once to play for a while with the boy, and the other, at night, To Play for a While With Me. So far I've got no complaints, nor have I heard Anyone in the UBPC or the Sugar Complex complain that He's neglecting his responsibilities. His children don't worry me, nor his grandchildren, who live here more than in his house, because they're Thrilled to have an Uncle who can't even talk. Not to mention that their grandmother, when she gets Fed Up with them, sends them over to me yelling "Go bother your Thirty-Year-Old Grandma a while, and play with your Newborn Uncle!" at the top of her lungs so all El Batey can hear. That's what everybody calls my baby: "The Uncle." At first it bothered me, but now, sometimes I call him Uncle myself.

Translation by Dick Cluster

Unplugged

Eduardo del Llano

I've left the country.

Spread the word. Make a big splash. Let everyone know.

Is that supposed to be a dare? No, it's more like I'm begging. Please, say it loud and clear to friend and foe; tell them Nicanor O'Donnell, the writer, is living in Europe now.

But keep this part to yourselves. The first day, Rodríguez slipped a videocasette into my hand.

"Be sure to watch it tonight, there's a line," he said, vanishing into the crowd of ice cream lovers at Coppelia.

I watched it that night. It was a revolting teleplay—Venezuelan, or Colombian, or Puerto Rican, or else some slick three-way co-production. I was insulted that Rodríguez felt he had a right to ruin my free time with something like that, even though if it hadn't been his revolting video, I'm sure I'd have watched something just as bad on TV.

"So," he prompted at nine the next morning, "that's really something, isn't it?"

With that, an inner voice yelled out to me that my friend expected an impassioned ode to his audiovisual material. I fished around for some positive-sounding equivalent of "disgusting, pathetic piece of crap" but right then, I had a hard time finding one.

"Don't tell me you didn't realize," he said. Then he explained that the actress playing the boy's mother was the one who had left Cuba about ten years ago, and that the boy himself (before he left too) had played one of the leads in that endless detective series that's apparently supposed to prove all cops are good-looking and smart. After he explained all that, he stood there looking at me as if he had said more than enough.

"Well, whaddya know," I declared

Then he asked me to get the video to Ana, a law student and mutual friend who lives near me. I didn't say no. I almost never do. Don't ask me why. That's like asking why kids always draw houses with sloping roofs.

"Thanks," Ana said, her face all twisted out of shape. "This whole country's got a toothache." She explained to me that in the dental wing of the polyclinic she went to, the compressor (whatever that was) had broken down, so they hadn't seen any new cases for two weeks now. That morning she had gone looking for other options.

"There's an epidemic of broken compressors in the polyclinics. I got the phone numbers of three private dentists, but one is out of town, the second overcharges and the third has no more openings this month."

She thanked me again for bringing the cassette; then she offered to lend me a book and said to read it in a hurry, because it belonged to her boyfriend. It was a novel by a woman writer who had emigrated some ten years earlier. That night I turned off the TV with a flourish, opting for literature instead. Ana's toothache was like a multiple orgasm compared to that novel. It was an endless succession of troubles, two hundred pages worth. Living through them all was hard enough, but even worse, they were boring.

The next morning this long-haired guy came to see me saying Ana had sent him. It was the boyfriend, of course. Five or six years ago, my body was a lot like his.

"And look at this," he said, pulling his wallet out of his bag and a folded paper out of his wallet. He handed it to me. It was a poem by another émigré writer, a poem that was part of a novel. The guy carried it around with him like a lucky charm, and he recited a piece from memory.

"That's the best picture ever painted of Havana."

"It's pretty good," I allowed, "but not the best."

We debated the point. The guy told me that in order to see something really clearly, you had to look at it from a distance. I cracked a joke about farsightedness, and he almost punched me out.

That afternoon I spotted Rodríguez from across the street. He was coming toward me carrying two more videos, so I ducked into the first available doorway. Turns out it was the entrance to a photography studio. A cleaning lady asked me what I wanted. I said I needed some passport pictures. They made me put down five dollars, which was all the capital I'd have until the next ice age. Then they ushered me into a closed cubicle, where they had me put on a piece of striped jacket and a tie Jimi Hendrix would have detested. I slicked my hair down, blinked and, naturally, that's just when the flashbulb went off. Then I left with a receipt in my pocket, and there stood my friend.

"When I saw you go in there, I waited for you so I could pass on some terrific material," he said. "And by the way, if you needed your picture taken, I could have arranged for a pal of mine to do it for free."

With that, he lent me not the videos, but a CD by a folk singer who, since leaving the island, has been doing more or less the same thing as before, only with fancier packaging.

"I can't stand the *punto guajiro*," I protested. I hate that music from out in the sticks.

"Just listen to it."

Later on that day, to the explosive accompaniment of Cuban lutes and bongoes, I gathered that God had something to tell me. So I got to thinking.

No one is a prophet in his own land. That's true enough. But in this case, something else was going on. When your average *compañero* reads the work of his fellow Cubans who have left for good, it's not so much for what they have to say—mostly, that's no news to anyone— but because the very act of reading a presumably unauthorized book makes you one of the enlightened few, a member of the sacred brotherhood of laid-back resisters. Reading that book and passing it on is an act of civil disobedience that's neither too serious nor too forbidden. That's where aesthetic battle lines blur: it's not a question of good émigré writers versus bad, but of writers who are good because they're émigrés. (And the fact that they look so sharp and pleasantly plump in those photos of theirs is one more point in their favor). There are radical readers who claim they limit their consumption to imports; they even search used book stores for whatever said writers may have left behind, then pour over old drafts looking for code words and hidden messages.

The same goes for music and audiovisuals. A trumpet solo by an émigré musician, or a documentary about insects, will always find some diehard willing to make copies and read things into them.

Anyhow, I thought all that and decided that besides giving me the chance to see how certain things are, God was hinting at a method. I had published a novel, *We, the Impotent,* two years earlier. It was well-received and even got a flattering review in one magazine. But the fact is, it only sold fifty copies.

If I wanted to be read, I had to leave.

So I did.

I've been cooped up at home for three months now. During the first month, I got five copies of my new novel into shape. Rodríguez gave me a hand with them; I had no choice but to ask him for help. He got someone to design and print a terrific cover that looks imported. He also arranged for the innards to be printed and found someone to do the binding. They turned out perfectly, with my picture on the back cover; we used that passport photo I had taken the day I ducked into the photo studio. When everything was ready, we recruited several friends for our little campaign, including Ana. Ana has turned me into an idol at the university; she also does my shopping. Her new boyfriend is a dentist.

Of course, becoming a shut in—imploding that way—is a tough sacrifice. It was reassuring to discover I had a predecessor, a character of Mark Twain's who faked his own death, anticipating that he would be revered as a great painter. And for him it was worth it. That's why the important thing now is to spread the word far and wide, to convince the world that I'm living in Paris and that Gallimard has brought out my novel in a deluxe edition with several printings. According to Rodríguez, those five copies are circulating like crazy. The method works. So, please, make a big splash.

I've just left my house for the first time. Naturally, I took the necessary precautions; I have on dark glasses and an Antz cap. Nevertheless, Rodríguez spotted me on the streetcorner.

"What the fuck do you think you're doing?" he yelled. "Do you want to ruin everything?"

I was too embarrassed to say I just wanted to buy a paper, so I said something about the light and the smell of flowers.

"Stop talking like a fruitcake. You're a celebrity now. If they recognize you, you'll screw up everything."

I felt an urge to rebel. A tiny little urge.

"Who's taking the chances here, anyhow? If I'm found out, it'll be my problem, won't it?"

He opened his mouth to answer me but then, he changed his mind. He was staring over my shoulder at something.

"Turn around slowly, and take a look at that guy coming out of the snack bar."

When I did, I could hardly keep from screaming. The fellow had on a hat and a raincoat, but I recognized him right off. I had seen his photo lots of times on shiny covers.

"He only lets himself leave the house once a year," Rodríguez said.

Translation by Louise B. Popkin

Dreams of Flying

Eduardo del Llano

and everything's fine until I wake up at an altitude of fifteen thousand feet. Terrified, all I can do is close my eyes and go back to sleep, but that's dangerous—preposterous, in fact. No one can actually fly while they're asleep, they just think they can. And no one can fly while they're awake either, so I begin to descend. When I'm about to crash, I discover I've been dreaming, which automatically upends all my earlier reflections. However, a few details remain murky: why is the earth still coming closer? How come I was able to soar to such heights at first, when I can't do that now? I opt for the only sensible solution—namely, falling asleep right before I land. In my dreams I finally hit the ground, but it's not the least bit painful. Then I realize that, strange as it sounds, I'm both awake and flying, and asleep, out cold. But when you come right down to it, that's not so bad. Why, you can even get used to it, as long as your arms don't get too tired.

Nicanor passed a row of empty doorways, a vacant lot and a gas station that looked like it belonged in the Sahara; but when he reached the warehouse he really needed to go, so he asked the watchman to let him in for a second, for God's sake. The watchman made him repeat his request three times and then said sure he would, except he'd have to ask his boss; with that, he went back through the huge rusty iron gate, which was still ajar. Nicanor stood there waiting with his legs crossed and his lower lip caught between his teeth. Finally the watchman came out with a guy who held out his hand and said he was Angel, the manager. Nicanor introduced himself as an art critic, saying pleased to meet you and I'm about to wet my pants.

"This is highly irregular," remarked the manager. "But I'll let you in, because I know how that can be. It's down the hall on your right, past the office and the pile of retreads."

Following the manager's directions, Nicanor came to a narrow place with an awful stench; it had a door which refused to close and sported a huge emblematic carving of a penis. Inside were a broken sink and two cubicles; he plunged into the nearest one, wading through lumpy liquids. Then he closed his eyes, thought simultaneously of Niagara and Vesuvius, took aim at a floating turd and in less than a second cut it in two.

"Aah," he declared. He was engrossed in the process of returning his male organ to its customary resting place, when the swinging door to the cubicle caught his eye. (Later he could have sworn that a ray of light came to guide him, perhaps even a transfigured glow, a gentle aura, emanating from the wood.) There was an area on its surface, among all the lewd carvings and incitements to fornication, where the veneer had come off. And right there on that barren stretch, he glimpsed some smudgy patches and an all-too-familiar signature.

"Holy shit," he said, tearing out of the cubicle before he could even zip up his fly.

"Salvador Dalí? You mean to tell me there's an original Dalí on a bathroom door in Guanabacoa?"

"A version of the *Burning Giraffe*," Nicanor clarified. "It's in terrible shape, but it's recognizable. And if I may say so, it's much better than the other one."

Rodríguez—the same Rodríguez who signs his name to the most impenetrable essays ever found in scholarly journals on art history and theory; author of the book *Champions of the Ideologeme*, member of the International Association of Critics and circumstances permitting, photographer of male nudes, to boot; Rodríguez, in sum, a dwarfish polyglot and fruitcake who, when he has a headache, just picks up any volume by Lyotard or Francastel—let out a semiotically pure guffaw and shook like an asthmatic.

"Come off it," he said. "You're more likely to find a copy of Aristotle's *Poetics* in the snack bar at the Council of State."

"It's a Dalí," Nicanor insisted, "but I need for you to see it, so I can be sure. Even though I'm sure now."

"My boy, Dalí never set foot in this country. He wasn't that much of a surrealist."

Nicanor sighed. He had come straight from the site of his national treasure to Rodríguez's place, certain that waiting to see him the next morning at the University would be tantamount to high treason. And now, that big peter puffer didn't believe him. Well, OK, then, he'd give it another try. He had always suspected that those guys who witness miracles and when they go to tell about it, get all worked up and start panting and spouting nonsense, have no one but themselves to blame when other people are skeptical.

"Who's to say Dalí didn't stop off here at some point? Or maybe the doors in that bathroom are imported. Look, Rodríguez, I know it sounds weird. If you go see it and you assure me it's a forgery, I promise that'll be the end of it. You're the top specialist in twentieth century European art. But damn it, trust me, will you?"

"And you say there's shit floating around in puddles there?"

"It's a bathroom in a warehouse. What do you expect?"

"Good thing that Dalí of yours isn't on the floor. This is nuts, Nicanor," said Rodríguez pulling a pocket diary out of who knows where. "Let's see now, on Tuesday and Wednesday I'll be at that event, on Thursday I have office hours, and on Friday, I'm scheduled to meet with the curator from the Birmingham Photo Gallery. On weekends, the warehouse is probably closed. Let's say I give you a call around the middle of . . ."

"Lend me your camera."

"The Nikon? Over my dead body."

"Come on, lend it to me. And I'll pose for you, whenever you want."

What was on the mind of Nicanor O'Donnell, professor and third-rate critic, as he headed back to the warehouse, camera in hand and poised for action? Actually, a number of things. As he got off the bus, he said something about showing certain unspecified bastards a thing or two. And more than likely, that's what was uppermost in his mind. When you get right down to it, the primary purpose of everything we do is to teach one or more bastards a lesson.

"Don't tell me you're about to wet your pants again," the watchman commented sarcastically. "Aren't there any better bathrooms around?"

"OK, this is the last time," Nicanor begged. He had decided to keep his discovery a secret. The watchman or Angel might be self-taught art historians, or maybe they even had degrees. No one knew better than Nicanor how hard it was to find a job after you graduated.

Angel subjected the critic to a brief interrogation.

" I see you brought a camera."

"I was doing some work at the museum."

"And you couldn't take a leak there?"

"I did. But I've got a kidney problem."

"It's almost closing time."

Angel finally authorized a second trip to the toilet, on the condition that he escort Nicanor all the way to the door.

"It's not that we don't trust you," he clarified. "It's that this is no ordinary tire warehouse. It may not look like much, but there's a group of Spaniards who want to . . ."

Nicanor splashed his way back to the cubicle and confirmed that the Dalí was still where it belonged. He peed noisily, so that Angel would hear him. Then he focused the lens and measured the light. Click click click.

"I heard the camera clicking," the manager informed him. "You're up to something weird. I don't want to see you back here again. And close your damn fly."

No sooner was the photo paper in the developing tray, than Rodríguez started turning pale. Then, limp-wristed and ecstatic, he threw his arms around Nicanor.

"It's a Dalí, all right. If that's not a Dalí, I swear I'll sleep with a woman. Here, Nicanor, let me give you a kiss."

"Get your hands off me. I already said you could photograph me in the nude. Don't push it."

"Of course," the expert mused a moment later, "I'd have to see it to be absolutely sure. I'd have to date it tentatively, describe its style and pictorial substance, and assign it to a period in his work. Otherwise, I can hardly write a scholarly paper and without a paper, nobody will believe me."

"Believe *you*?" Nicanor said. "I'm the one who found it. Look, we can both announce its discovery, but it has to be clear that I'm the one who found it. This is my big chance."

"OK, fine," Rodríguez conceded. "Don't get upset. We'll put both our names on the paper. Now, let's go over to the warehouse."

"It's probably closed by now. We can go tomorrow. Of course, you have that event . . ."

"They can take their event and shove it. Oh, Nicanor, come closer, let's celebrate. I'm so happy . . ."

"Enough is enough," Angel roared. He had a crowbar in his hand, and he was wielding it like a sword. "Beat it, or I'm calling the police."

"But my friend and I have the same kidney problem . . ."

"Yeah, I bet you two have the same problem. Damn it, it doesn't pay to be nice. First you show up here by yourself, next you bring a camera to take pictures of your gross weirdo stuff and now, you bring a friend. What do you think this is, anyhow?"

"Angel," said Nicanor, putting his hand in his pocket, "if you want, we'd be happy to show our appreciation . . . Come on, it's really urgent."

The crowbar shook menacingly.

"If it's all that urgent, go do it under some bushes. I don't want to discuss it any further. We're expecting an important visit from a group of Spaniards. So, take your hand out of there and get moving before I bust your brains out!"

Rodríguez pulled on Nicanor's arm.

"Drop it. Come on, let's go."

Angel watched them leave, still brandishing his cautionary crowbar.

The watchman chuckled.

"Artists do the damndest things."

Two days later, Nicanor walked into the National Library and headed straight for the table where Rodríguez was sitting.

"I've found an old man who was a custodian at the warehouse back in the fifties, when the place was part of the Sánchez pharmacy chain. I showed him a picture of Dalí, and it rang a bell. He let him use the bathroom once. Dalí had problems with diarrhea . . ."

"That guy must be at least eighty by now. I'm not sure he's a reliable witness."

"The old man is perfectly fine. I taped him and took a few snapshots. He says Dalí had a little satchel with him. I bet he kept some tubes of paint in there. You know how it is with diarrhea. He was stuck in that bathroom, he saw the door, and he figured he might as well paint a little doodad . . . I can just picture him."

Rodríguez nodded slowly.

"Well, there is a period of a few weeks in Dalí's biography, precisely during those years, when he's unaccounted for . . . so that may be. From what I can see in the photos, it was painted in a hurry; the brushstrokes are very fluid. And it does anticipate the new figuration of the sixties. Oh, Nicanor, that lousy giraffe is worth its weight in gold. The tough part is, I can't stick my neck out unless I actually see the door. We'll have to go back to . . ."

"Look, I already told you," Nicanor replied, "don't even think about it. If we talk to the manager of the warehouse, he'll see to it we get screwed; or even worse, he'll try to take all the credit himself. Which is exactly what will happen if we go through the Ministry of Culture. The only thing we can do is what we discussed."

"But that's nuts. We'll be asking for trouble."

"No, we'll be safeguarding a national treasure. Either we steal that door or any day now, someone's going to carve a bare-assed lady right over the giraffe. Come on, Rodríguez, make up your mind or I'll have to do it by myself."

Rodríguez made his mind up the next day, when he read in the paper that a Spanish firm had signed an agreement with the government to create a mixed venture for the production of tires. The Spaniards would supply startup capital for the renovation and reopening of the company's run down facilities, and they would make use of abandoned buildings, especially old warehouses, as the sites for additional new ones. "Our first job is to clean up, decorate and repaint," declared the head of the company earnestly, "you can't expect to motivate people without a genuine work aesthetic."

"If they don't toss that door and put up a new one, we'll know they're on to the giraffe," whimpered the expert. "Remember, Dalí was Spanish. One spic with a belly ache and we could lose everything. You were right, Nicanor. We've got to beat them to it."

To throw them off track, Nicanor went straight to a show by a small-town artist and published a review about it the following day, three paragraphs on the next to last page of the paper. In his classes, he avoided glowing references to surrealism or twentieth century art in general. Rodríguez met with the English curator and made a point of dismissing the vanguard movements out of hand. "My thing is postmodern iconic resemantization," he commented. "That should be obvious from my published work."

On Friday night, Nicanor called Rodríguez to say that Picasso had always been a creep. That was their signal.

"There's a way in through the back," Nicanor explained. "And we can use this iron to jimmy the lock. The watchman will never know the difference."

They had parked the car on the corner, about fifty yards from there. It was Rodríguez's car, of course. On the way over, they put on some black gloves.

"We should have brought along a door that's in decent shape to replace the one on the cubicle," the expert remarked. "Angel or the watchman is bound to suspect us, when they realize someone took it."

"They have no idea why we care about that bathroom. Or, to be more precise, they have the wrong idea. I don't think they'll notice anything missing tomorrow. What on earth could be more natural than a cannibalized toilet? Besides, we'll be lucky to get out of there with a door. Let's not push our luck by trying to get one in."

Forcing the back entrance wasn't hard. Rodríguez kept an eye out, while Nicanor pried open the lock. One average click and they discovered that the night outside wasn't all that dark.

"Get out the flashlight."

"It's on already. Thing is, I had to use the batteries from the radio."

Making it down the hallway, which reeked of burnt plastic, was like walking a tightrope. They inched their way carefully past piles of tires, wooden boxes and cartons, old machines and puddles of grease. Even so, Rodríguez tripped over something and fell; he sounded like a piano coming down on a heap of saws.

"Maybe I didn't make myself clear," said Nicanor. "The whole idea is that the watchman shouldn't hear us."

"Sorry," Rodríguez stammered. "Mother of God, are we ever nuts."

One way or another, Nicanor managed to find his way to the bathroom. He heaved a sigh of relief as first his nose, then the flashlight, informed him he was wading through familiar puddles of filth. He located the cubicle, opened the door and tried his best to sound ceremonious:

"Rodríguez, look at this."

The painting looked pretty beat up, but the giraffe and the signature were still there. For a brief moment, the glow from the flashlight took on the golden hue of Fra Angelico's halos.

"My God," the expert murmured. "What a treasure. It really is Dalí."

"What did I tell you. Now, hang on to the door, will you? Steady, like a man."

Nicanor pried off the first hinge. And the second. Then they heard a noise that wasn't theirs.

"It's the watchman. Hurry up, there's only one to go."

"Hold on."

There were footsteps out in the hall. Wary, anxious footsteps belonging to one person. A voice asked who was in there.

"There's still another hinge," whispered Nicanor. "Pay attention. Now is no time for cold feet."

"Don't forget I'm a faggot," said Rodríguez.

A dark silhouette appeared at the entrance to the bathroom. Nicanor barked an order and with a single tug, they tore the swinging door off the cubicle; then they rushed at the watchman, surrealist shield in hand.

Bam.

They were barely out of there when the first shot rang out. The watchman must not have appreciated being stepped on and poked in the eye with a corner of the door. He fired another shot. Nicanor and Rodríguez made it to the back entrance, now an exit, and escaped into the darkness.

A passerby, or someone with just enough time to look out the window, would have seen a wooden rectangle with two pairs of legs running into the wind and climbing into a Lada 1600, while some guy chased after them with a hand over one eye, carrying on and firing a gun. That's all. It wasn't much, and the police officer who showed up twenty-five minutes later had a pretty hard time finding witnesses.

Rodríguez burst into tears, cried for about half an hour and was still crying when Nicanor put his arm around him and gave him a little peck on the ear.

"If he had . . . hit me . . . damn it, I wouldn't care. But this . . . just breaks . . . my . . . heart."

The door lay on top of a table, in the middle of the room. There were two holes in it: one had beheaded the giraffe and the other had left the painting without a signature. What's more, a tiny crack that had appeared when the last hinge came off now extended over fully half of its museum-quality surface.

"It's not too late to do something," said Nicanor half-heartedly.

"There's . . . nothing we can . . . do. A famous painting can be restored, but first you have to prove . . . it's . . . famous. If we show up at the National Museum with this, they'll just laugh at us, same as if we try to sell it . . . to a . . . foreign . . . collector. Our national treasure is kaput. And we'll be . . . going to . . . jail . . . for sure. God, we really are nuts . . ."

But Nicanor wasn't about to give in.

"It's not fair. We didn't go risking our necks over a shitty old broken down door. If they don't come after us in a few days, go ahead and write that paper. This is still our big chance. Let's try and convince all those bastards we've got a Dalí."

"You don't get it, do you? We'll just be wasting our time and asking for trouble. God, why didn't I run off with that German? By now I'd have gotten a sex change and a new name. I'd be . . . Ana. I've dreamed about being Ana since I was a kid."

"You still can be. You're famous, and you're always going off on trips. I'm the one who's really screwed."

"I'm too old for that, Nicanor. Too old and too tied down here. That German was the love of my life."

"Oh, you're just in a snit. Are you going to write that paper or aren't you?"

Rodríguez burst into tears again and shook his head no. Nicanor felt like hugging him, smashing his head against the floor, crying with him and then committing suicide. What he did instead was start taking his clothes off.

"If you write that paper and hang in with me while we give it a shot . . ."

Rodríguez looked at him, still sniveling.

"I said I'd pose for you, didn't I? Well, here I am. Take my picture . . . Ana."

The police hardly investigated, since they couldn't get terribly worked up over two burglars breaking into a warehouse to make off with nothing but the door from a bathroom cubicle. They found no fingerprints, and the witnesses couldn't even agree on the color of the getaway car. Moreover, with his memory affected by the attack, the watchman's account was none too coherent. From what he said, it wasn't clear if the object in question had been stolen, or it had decided to leave on its own after poking him in the eye. The new heads of the company promptly replaced both the watchman and the door.

Nicanor and Rodriguez waited a week, then tried, cagily and unsuccessfully, to establish the authenticity of the Dalí. All they got for their efforts was a reputation as a couple of lunatics. The "lunatics" part wasn't true; the "couple" part eventually was. One day, in a fit of rage, the two of them went at the painting, scratching and defacing it by carving phalluses and slogans on it. After that, everything returned to normal and to this day, the bastards can read reviews by one and the other in scholarly journals and the press.

Nicanor is now Rodríguez's only model. Mostly, he poses as a bird, or as Icarus. When you come right down to it that's not so bad; why, you can even get used to it, as long as your arms don't get too tired.

Translation by Louise B. Popkin

The Man from Nowhere

Miguel Mejides

For my father

Some people always go against the grain, but I don't go against anything. That may stem from the great handicap that's marked my life: I'm cross-eyed. Ever since I could think, since the first time I studied myself in the mirror and saw my eyes, I told myself I was a man destined for silence and meditation, for smiling and long walks through the city I'd one day choose for my solitary life.

My mother, thank God, always understood I was the quiet type, like a mute songbird. Likewise, she came to accept my decision to head out of our little town and make something of myself in Havana. I've never been able to shake the image of her seeing me off at the train station, waving a linen hankie in farewell, the train smoke all around her and the saintly smile she never lost, not even in death.

Havana affects me the same way. See how it's rained these last few years. Until not long ago I enjoyed surveying Havana with the same gaze I had when I first arrived, back in January, 1990, when the city still retained a haze of lights and mysteries. The bus entered by way of the old main highway, continued toward the statue of the Virgin of the Road and straight down Luyano Street. At the end of my journey, I was awe-struck by the statue of our poet-hero, Jose Marti, in Revolution Square and by the twinkling Ferris wheel in the amusement park across from the bus terminal.

I'll never forget the taxi that took me to Infanta 234, a bright orange DeSoto with the coat-of-arms of some age-old Spanish province and the number 13 painted on the door. The driver was a short geezer with an Andalusian accent, wearing a colorful hat.

"That's the place," he said, flashing his stained teeth.

When I paid him, he got a good look at me and his eyes widened in alarm. "Buy yourself some specs," he told me.

My Aunt Buza greeted me half-solicitous, half-surprised. She gave me the same look the taxi driver had and spoke of charms that cured eye diseases. Her husband was in a bad mood and he asked if I knew how to drive. When I said no, he talked about modern times, how a man at the turn of this century has to know how to get around by car. Then he discussed in detail the interview I'd undergo the next morning.

"Just talk about the basics, don't blow your nose, and lie: say you know how to drive."

I still have no idea what that had to do with the job I was applying for. That night they settled me in a small room next to the kitchen. Its only charm was a large window looking out on Havana. Everything was so different from my home town. I was struck by the city's traffic and the sea—which I guessed was on the horizon of the night sky—and the Progreso Radio Building across the street, where soap operas were born, the love stories that made Mom sigh. I'm in Havana, I said, and I'll never turn my back on its flame. This town could shower you with pleasure one minute and turn into hell the next.

But since I was in that grieving phase (I don't know if I'll ever come out of it), the interview was a disaster. At eight in the morning, we planted ourselves by the manager's office at the Hotel Nacional. I was so nervous, I told my aunt's husband I needed to go the bathroom. He pointed out the way and when I glanced in the mirror, I saw that my eyes had never crossed so hard. I was afraid my pupils would fall out of their sockets and into the sink.

When I got back, they were waiting for me. The manager ushered us into his office. He was about 30 and had a mole on his nose. He said something about Greek beauty, about the Greek ideal of beauty, and that hotels were the palaces of kings.

"I'm sure you understand, Jeronimo," he said abruptly.

"Maybe if he wore dark glasses no one'd notice," my aunt's husband said.

"But he can't wear them at night. A hotel is a living organism," he said with conviction. "If just one body is out of sync, that beauty is spoiled."

On the way back, I recalled what the taxi driver had said. I decided that, first chance I got, I'd buy a pair of glasses. My mother had convinced her sister that Jeronimo could come up with a job for me at the Hotel Nacional where he'd worked since he was a teenager. My mother had failed to mention my crossed eyes. She'd sent many photos of me, just my profile, as if I were the best looking guy in the world. My eyes would force me to go back home. They'd force me to grow old in that little piece of the world where a cemetery marks the turn-off to the only road connecting it to Camaguey.

"Stay a week, if you like, and then buy a ticket back," Aunt Buza said.

"There're no opportunities back home," I said.

"In those tiny towns, people get used to diseases like yours," she pronounced.

That very afternoon, I bought glasses from a street vendor in Galiano. They weren't high quality, but you had to look hard to detect my eyes. With my new look, I spent all my time walking around Havana. By 7 AM sharp, I'd already hit the streets. First I walked around El Cerro; then Marianao. By the time I started my trek down Carlos III, more than a week had gone by. I wasn't much trouble to my aunt and uncle. I didn't turn on the lamp at night, I rarely relieved myself in their bathroom, and in the morning I just had coffee. When I returned in the dead of night, I ate whatever leftovers were on the stove. I sincerely hoped to find work so I could stay in Havana. But everywhere people looked at me funny and told me they had no openings. A month went by like that and my aunt's patience wore thin. I recall the night I tiptoed in and didn't find any food. In place of the usual pan, there was a no nonsense note saying they'd bought me a train ticket for the next morning. That's when I realized I was on my own in Havana.

Without any fuss, I picked up my suitcase and set off. I went to Prado Park and stretched out on a marble bench in front of the Hotel Seville. The laurel trees were the best cover for my derelict state. I set my suitcase at my feet and settled down to sleep, my hands crossed behind my neck. I was just drifting off when I heard voices coming from the roots of the laurel trees. It was a diatribe on the last Christmas, about the curse the city was having to come to terms with.

"Who's there?" I managed to say.

I thought about how hunger can make you hallucinate. Yet that seemingly endless conversation soothed me. The voices were coming from a sonorous cone. The conversation was drowned out by a snicker that went on and on.

"Hey! Are you fish, angels, or what?" I shouted.

I flopped down next to a laurel, put my ear to its roots, and heard the Glenn Miller band playing "String of Pearls." I lay there for a long time, my face resting on the ground. Later, I made out a devilish laugh and a monologue that seemed otherworldly.

"That hive of humanity that lives up top, that Havana that's slave to the light will raise a monument to our catechistic labor some day, a monument to our galleys that sail the furrows of the earth, a monument to our warehouses crammed with salt and coffee, cured meat and garlic, our galleys brimming with the priesthood of commerce and good service, full of the lively noise of the world . . ."

Just then I clearly made out the scraping sound of my suitcase being snatched from the Prado bench. I saw two people running off into the distant night on the street next to the Hotel Seville. Laughter echoed from under the earth. I said one of those words you only utter when you're miserable. My voice was drowned out by the thunderous blare of the jazz band . . .

I didn't sleep that night. I spent the night walking around the Prado and Central Park. Many believe that being cross-eyed makes you see objects in a different dimension. But I saw the city the way it really looks. I'd observed Havana for a month and now detected the danger. There was no public lighting. All I could make out was the marquee of the Hotel Inglaterra. The Garcia Lorca Theater looked like a sylph's castle. The Payret Theater billboard lifted Catherine Deneuve high overhead. The Capitol building was the ultimate mirror of the city. Central Park mimicked an ordinary day when people come out to talk on and on about scandals. Blacks in guarachera shirts looked ready for Carnival. Women in dresses cut by pious seamstresses on Monte Street strolled down shadowy trails. Sodomites tattooed trees with men's hearts and night owls lost extravagant bets on the illegal Chinese lottery.

And there I was, walking around the forbidden city, my hunger following the aromas, my gut somersaulting. Up walked a mulatto man pushing his sweets.

"Come on, big shot, buy yourself a nice piece of rum cake."

I mumbled like a fool, "Pains and misfortunes."

I was thinking about what I'd just said, how I'd heard my mother use that saying about mankind's luck. About how Havana was so different from my town, how foreign the night sounds were. My town didn't have night owls, just early birds taking the train to Camaguey. And the great city was a shop window for people who rejected the law of daylight hours, people living in tenements dark as a cave, in shacks where fathers discovered their daughters' young beauty early on, shacks where you never saw the sky, where the sun was a curse to the laws of the switchblade and blood, the laws of Old Havana, a Havana designed for carriages and slaves, for lights from bitter firewood, a city that still had to come to grips with the workings of the modern era.

And in the farthest corner of the park, a dingy little kiosk, with little or no signs of life, where a little old man bought and sold old magazines. Nat King Cole singing at the Tropicana; Che Guevara with his visionary eyes; Camilio Cienfuegos, a revolutionary hero astride a horse of one hundred waters; the 1962 missile crisis; Khrushchev pointing out a black star . . . People buying magazines that were the biographies of their souls. And me, fleeing from that experience, from the photos that at once had no connection to my life and yet did. Wandering past the doorways of the tobacco factories with the rustling of fine Pinar del Rio tobacco leaves, the murmuring of binnacles that housed Romeo and Juliet, Partaga, and Montecristo cigars. Searching for Prado Park again, down sleepy, crumbling paths, and now in the park, passing the time until morning, then taking my train to the vegetal world of the province, returning to my mother, to the routine of taking a piss, then going to bed at ten. To the oppression of obedience and pretense.

Finally I came back to the marble bench where they had stolen my suitcase, the laurel tree humbled now by the absence of Glenn Miller's music.

"Get your peanut brittle here!" shouted a dwarf on the same corner of the Hotel Seville. Repeating his patter like someone about to slit his wrists. "Hey, kid, peanut brittle!" he shouted at me from over there. I wanted to tell him I didn't have a cent. I felt like the biggest lowlife, nothing could save me, especially the train taking me far from Havana. Then the dwarf crossed the street and planted himself right in front of me, smiling, wearing a corduroy cap, huge shoes and muslin trousers.

"Here," he held out a peanut bar and told me he was headed home. "Come on, come on, eat it." I dug into it, as he watched me and I watched him too.

"Who buys your wares at night?" I asked him.

"No one. Nighttime amuses me."

And off he went, hawking his wares. "Everybody's crazy around here," I muttered and looked down the deserted streets. All you could hear was a far off voice coming from the top of the Hotel Seville, the voice of a woman wailing, out of the loneliness boleros tell of and someone, also a woman I think, trying to calm her in a low voice. I fell asleep for a little while, more than a little while.

I awoke with crow shit splattered like a corn tortilla next to me. I looked at the critter and thought, how ironic. The sun was coming up and the crow looked like burnished tar. Sparrows were flying out of their hideaways, too, to start their nameless battles in the laurels. I felt around in my pocket and found my ticket to Camaguey, the ticket that would take me away from my hope. I started to walk to the station and saw that the Prado had suddenly come to life. Crowds of people scurried from one side of the park to the other, not heading anywhere in particular, lined up at bus stops to board nonexistent buses. There wasn't one restaurant, no smell of coffee along the way. As day broke that morning, the city was just a point on the map with no aromas, only a fresh breeze blowing from the sea. Just the smell of that sea waking up.

"God exists," said a woman in her fifties as she passed by me, very close to the station.

"So does the devil," I said, not giving her another thought.

In rapid succession, I showed my ticket to the guard at the door to the station lobby, then stood at the ticket window, holding out my ID card, my laminated photo, the one with my eyes crossed, so they could verify the ticket was mine. The woman looked at my eyes, then at the eyes in the photo, checking my ID number, like the brand on some tame bull, my height in inches, my mouth's nervous tick, my travel permit.

"The train leaves early," the woman said. "Go to platform three, coach 52, seat 81. If you're traveling with food, it may be confiscated, no animals allowed, all travelers must . . ."

I quit listening and walked to the entrance to platform three where someone asked for my ticket and demanded to see my ID card again. This time it was a short, fat man with a gray mustache. Finally, with a little shove, he let me pass, and I ran down the platform, with that fear I have of arriving late to places. What about coach 52? All the others cars were there, not mine. I started to yell. A crowd of about 30 people grouped around me. The locomotive whistled its final warning. "Coach 52?!!!!!!!!" I demanded. The fat man came up and said that because of an unpardonable error they hadn't hooked up coach 52. In a wheezy voice, he informed us that the price of the ticket would be refunded and we'd leave the next morning. I drew up to my full height and said I wanted to see the administrator, someone, to demand coach 52. The man pulled on his mustache and said that given the imperialistic blockade, one must have a conscience, a spirit of sacrifice. Travel tomorrow, folks.

I decided not to pursue it. No one would pay attention to me. I returned to the ticket window where the same woman read me the handbook on travelers' responsibilities and refunded the price of my ticket. Barely twenty pesos. I made a decision—1 would stay in Havana. Perhaps my destiny was here with two million souls facing the Gulf of Mexico. What's the difference if I died in hock? Who cares about a cross-eyed guy? Who'd cry for a cross-eyed guy? Only my mother would suffer, but she'd get over it. Just like when Papa died. Days of grieving, of mourning, and then Christian resignation.

I left the station, headed nowhere in particular. I was convinced—l've always suffered from fantasies—that someone would feel sorry for me. In the meantime, where should I go? Hunger kept on pummeling my stomach. With my twenty pesos I figured I'd eat one of those fish fritters they sell on Puerto Avenue. I just had to go down a couple of winding alleys and I'd be there in no time. As I was about to set off, I saw on the same corner where they parked the rental cars, on the sewer culvert that jutted out into the street like a metallic helmet, the dwarf who had given me the peanut brittle at dawn. He recognized me and waved his corduroy cap. I went over to him and was really surprised when I saw him muttering angrily. He said something about kids, how you couldn't recruit today's youth, that the hidden people will dwindle in number, that the Grail would have to import creatures from another planet.

"What're you talking about?" I asked him.

"Nothing," he answered. "An old dwarf's crazy ideas."

Like before, he handed me a peanut bar. I admit I was grateful for it, but I craved something else. Still I gobbled it down with the same savage appetite and he asked me where I was headed. I told him what had happened to me and about my resolve to stay in Havana.

He suddenly asked, "Do you have the guts to work for a dwarf?"

"Tell me what to do and I'll start right this minute," I said.

"I'll take a chance on you," he added.

I was going to tell him I was an honest man, when the dwarf squatted down, slid down the culvert and, somehow, maybe by magic, he reappeared dragging a package, looking every direction, carefully selecting his words.

"Someone we thought was reliable was supposed to take this package to 111 Aramburu Street. I can't budge from this corner, maybe one day you'll understand. I'm confident you can carry out this mission, your future depends on it."

He paused, took off his cap, scratched his head, and spoke about the forces that rule the underground, the palaces King Solomon built in the interior of the cities after his death, populated cities or in the ones that haven't been built yet.

"Take it or leave it."

I hoisted up the package and felt it rattle like a box filled with treasure. I was about to say something but the dwarf interrupted me.

"Sausages! Harmless sausages!" he repeated, overcome by a strange giddiness. "Be very careful. At the first sign of trouble, toss the package at the police's feet, that way they won't follow you."

And so the dwarf launched me on my first shady venture. Of course, my nerves were on edge as I went down the street. Each time I saw a policeman, I was ready to ditch the blessed sausages at his feet. But I got to Aramburu Street without a hitch. I rang the bell at number 111 and an old couple opened the door. They grilled me about a password I knew nothing about. I explained it was my first day as a delivery boy. They said when I visited them I should say, "Pontius Pilate!" Then, they led me to the living room and opened the package. It was thirty-odd cans of frankfurters.

"Here," the old lady said to me. I saw two twenty dollar bills and two ones. Pleased with myself, I returned to the train station but found no trace of the dwarf. One of the taxi drivers told me he'd seen the dwarf get into a blue car. I didn't know what to do with the money. It was way past noon by then and I all wanted to do was eat, sit down at a table and gorge myself, something I hadn't done since I left home. With that in mind, I went down to Puerto Avenue, by way of Central Park and the Prado, not taking the short cuts through Old Havana, which at that hour were covered by a fiery heat that consumed the street corners.

After bargaining with a woman in the shadows of a colonial doorway on Park Avenue, I bought a fritter and a tamarind drink at black market prices. Next I walked around the souvenir shops by the Cathedral. I was fascinated by cigarette lighters with scenes of Havana, American cigarettes, ballpoint pens that showed naked woman when you shook them, racks of fashion magazines from all over the world . . . All the while I asked myself why we were so isolated from the world. The archipelago, the island, was like a ship adrift that fled from commercial kitsch, explaining itself in a retro rhetoric, a rhetoric that's also kitsch. Next, I went to the Bodeguita de Medio and walked through it; in the bathroom I wrote my name in fancy Persian calligraphy and left. I went back to Central Park and watched the Catherine Deneuve movie in the Payret Theater.

When I came out, it was late afternoon so I went down to the port again. In the Dos Hermanos Bar, I ordered a double shot of rum with the little money I had left. From the bar I could see the ferries to Regla and Casa Blanca transporting passengers. In the Dos Hermanos people did some serious drinking. The longshoremen were knocking back a bottle of that infernal rum as if it were water, the bartender shouted the orders in a lingo I didn't understand, and the women who came in looked like they'd walked right out of some Japanese comic book, wearing dresses so tight they looked like badly rolled cigars.

"Take off those specs," one of them said provocatively, fawning on me. She was must have been close to 35, a half Chinese mulatta, pleasant to look at. She'd gotten fat and her hips were too round. Tourists no longer sought her out, passed her over in the game of international flags of love.

"I'm cross-eyed," I told her bravely. I lowered my glasses and she looked at my eyes, examined them, and talked about how cross-eyed people bring luck. She touched my head as if to exorcise her bad luck. In a very loud voice she said something like, "Hey, this guy's cross-eyed!" Two more women came over and touched my head, too. The bartender was generous and filled my glass. A black longshoreman came over and talked about the blind virgin, how there's a church in Guanabacoa, on the outskirts of the village, in the mountain, on the edge of the jungle, there's a hermitage where a virgin lives, they say she's from Toledo and can cure eye diseases. When he left, the Chinese mulatta said the black guy's a big windbag. She ordered a drink and got the bartender to fill my glass again.

"So, does the virgin exist?" I asked.

"God knows if she does, God only knows . . ." she said to me.

To make a long story short, I have to confess I tied on the biggest bitch of a drunk in my life. At ten I left with port dwellers and that riot of women in between tricks, everyone hugging me, touching my head. With so much alcohol everywhere I turned, I barely managed to hang on to those forty-two dollars, and since the dwarf hadn't showed up, they were my only lifesaver. In that condition, we walked down Puerto Avenue and left the port authority behind. In front of the Commercial Market, one of the longshoremen, the shortest one, a cocky guy from the Canaries, started to shout the name of Obdulio Miraverde, bookkeeper at the warehouse. He was telling me, breathing into my eyes, how the guy threw himself off the golden cupola on account of some lousy five hundred pesos that they'd stolen from the cash box, afraid they'd blame him for the theft.

"You don't understand, you cross-eyed piece of shit! He killed himself for 500 little pieces of paper with Marti's face on them!" He was shouting now. "He was my friend! Look, there's his ghost," he took me by the chin. "Look, there's Obdulio, reenacting his leap every night at midnight."

And the Chinese mulatta at my side, sticking her tongue in my eyes, like a windshield wiper, her tongue in my ear, between my teeth, my tongue and hers, the party, the mulatta's tongue, the suicide, the alcohol. And now out on the Point, with the fortress El Morro and its lighthouse in front of us, her hand down my pants, shaking me like a flask of elixir, me overflowing, in plain view of Havana, the coral horizon of lights, the chimerical city, and me with my traitorous barb. "Come on, soak me, fill my hand with your suds," she repeated and me, thinking about that dame, about Havana, about the jolt that left a stain on my pants like a map of the jungle.

Suddenly the idea of leaving popped into my head—to go to the Prado and get over my hangover. Without warning I started to run, I left the Malecon boardwalk behind, that barrier between the sea and the souls of the city. Not stopping till I was in front of the Hotel Seville, taking refuge in its doorway, next to the dwarf with his corduroy cap, his table loaded down with peanut brittle. And he, seeing the strange trance that had come over me, said to me, "Kid! Hey, kid!" And me, talking about the virgin who cures bad eyes, that virgin in Guanabacoa, the virgin from Toledo. Demanding to know if she exists, repeating, almost rudely, since I didn't know or remember his name: "Hey, dwarf. You. Dwarf. Over there. Come over here, dwarf . . ." Until he held out the third peanut bar in less than a day and I took a bite, and he brought up the money I'd been paid, and I dug around in my pocket and gave him the 42 dollars. He took the bills and held them up in the moonlight, looked them over, inspected them, and handed me back two dollars, your pay, hee, hee, hee, hee, hee, your first pay as a man. And I started to vomit, splattered the dwarf's muslin pants, the life went out of me and in the midst of all that, the dwarf kept saying: "They call me Pascualito. Don't drink any more, you can't do that in our business." At that, I went over to my bench, rolled around on the marble and stretched out like a snake. The dwarf shouted from the corner, "Meet me at the station tomorrow. Don't let me down." Once again I spewed a bilious, black, lumpy soup onto the laurel roots, listening to the dialog coming from under the earth, someone belting out a psalm about vegetables and grains, and Glenn Miller. And I fell asleep thinking about the crow shit that would wake me up at daybreak.

The next day I met the dwarf at the station. He told me he expected my approval any minute. "The Grail gets together in the mornings and hands out permits," he told me solemnly. We passed the time discussing my future. Pascualito insisted I should buy myself some new clothes, get rid of that shirt only a hick going nowhere would wear. They said something from under the culvert. I guess it was OK. Pascualito patted me on the back and said, I'm never wrong about people, I don't get mixed up with riffraff. He handed me a chit for the shop in the Hotel Seville. "Ask for Carmen Rosa, she'll fix you up with some clothes." Then he handed me a letter of introduction so they'd lease me a room in the crumbling building that had been a hotel and a Packard dealership in the forties.

"You'll live like a Christian there. I'll come by tonight and we can talk over your future."

This was the most radical change in my life. I bought clothes at the shop in the Hotel Seville and then went to the Packard dealership where a sad woman in a lacy, monogrammed blouse met me. She told me I'd share a room with Jeremias Batista. "He's downright crazy," she warned me; furthermore, the city housing authority was not responsible for lost articles. No women after 11 PM.

"Here's your key."

The room was no great shakes. It had two beds, a couple of night stands, a tall armoire, and a bathroom with a very large bathtub that was sitting on steel beams. The towel rack was decorated with the goddess Minerva, or so they said. The fact that the rain and the noise from the busy street below came in through cracks in the walls worried me. "But what more can I ask for? Just two days ago I was sleeping in the park and today I have clean clothes and a bed. I can even take a shower," I thought. Happiness is never complete, as you'll see. The water had to rise six floors to get to my room. But it was better than the park and the crow that shat at dawn.

At seven that evening, Pascualito came to the door and called out, "Five lights for Pontius Pilate." When I opened the door, he gave me a heart-felt "Hurrah!" He praised my good taste in clothes and told me I'd start work the very next morning. From his back pants pocket he took out a map of Havana and unrolled it on one of the beds. Cheerfully he said the city was divided up into business districts, where the sewer culverts were located. With a pen he marked the corner of 23rd and 12th, the Colon Cemetery and the Falla Bonet Mausoleum, the corner the Hotel Seville was on, the corner of Tejas, the rental car parking lot at the train station, the Virgin of the Road Statue, the League for the Prevention of Blindness, the Rumba Palace on Playa Street, 70th Street in Miramar. After marking a couple dozen points on the map, he leaned back and said he was happy I had been approved as a messenger for the Congregation. He apologetically informed me I'd been thoroughly investigated and that they knew about my mother, my Aunt Buza and her husband and my school days. Everything suggested I was trustworthy.

"From now on you're one of us. You'll be paid punctually, with bonuses for extra effort. You'll regulate the city and its needs. You'll have Havana at your feet because you'll be the link between the promises of the underground and the humans above."

"And who are you all?" I asked.

"Don't worry about that, it's not important . . ." he said. "Tomorrow you'll start your trips under Jeremias Batista's orders. Your password is five lights for Pontius Pilate. Every time you knock at a door or talk to me, say: "Five lights for Pontius Pilate!"

I walked him to the door, he shook my hand and, as he was leaving, he turned back to me and said, "The Virgin of the Eyes does exist, one day I'll take you to her sanctuary in Guanabacoa."

At eight I was in the dining room. The food was bad, but I ate it gratefully. I considered seeing a movie at the America Theater in Galiano. Then I gave up and decided to head off to bed. I thought about how this vast city gave me a better welcome than I'd foreseen. True, my new path was illegal. But who could live an honest life? I was a humble supplier of merchandise. Surely God would grace me with His pardon.

In the room, I met Jeremias Batista. He was in his skivvies, muttering, cutting his toenails. I introduced myself and he said he knew who I was. I was going to ask how but he interrupted me, asserting that the dwarves knew a lot. He declared the following:

"All that glitters is not gold. I can't tell you more than that, the rest you'll learn for yourself. I carry my orders out to the tee. Tomorrow we'll start by passing out the beef. I'll get straight to the point about being roommates—1 like to sneak street walkers in here. When I do, you take a hike. I don't like farting. I don't like people who snore or have long toenails. One more thing. Learn everything you can about this fucking city or you won't be any use to the business. I'll wake you up at 3 AM."

And he really did get me up at that hour and we quickly headed for the Virgin of the Road Statue. There we took our positions, barely speaking a word. At nearly dawn a truck pulled up loaded with cattle. Jeremias Batista chatted with the driver then suddenly Pascualito materialized through a culvert, along with half a dozen other dwarves. Without raising his voice once, Pascualito ordered them to open the back of the truck. Then they prodded the cows until they jumped into the void of the culvert. In a while all that was left was the unmistakable odor of animal fear on the pavement.

"It's like there's a relic down there you have to offer sacrifices to," Jeremias commented.

That day, till nightfall, we went back and forth as messengers. So it went every Friday, slaughter day. Saturdays and Wednesdays you parceled out canned meats. There was hardly any work to do on Sundays. Mondays started the work week with orders for clothes. Tuesdays were catch-all days and you could be loaded down with anything from an elephant to a package of needles. Thursdays were medical days; we circulated medications around Havana that came from the pantheon of the Falla Bonet Mausoleum in Colon. You carried a lot of money around and soon Jeremias taught me to make the most of that. We sold the dollars we'd just been paid in the afternoon, and bought them back cheaper in Trillo Park at night. You added these riches to the bonuses Pascualito handed out on the corner of the Hotel Seville.

I was getting rich so I bought myself a walkman, some cowboy boots, flowered shirts and a new pair of glasses. I started sending my mother an allowance and it looked like I'd go on like that forever. Late at night I went dancing in the discos and there I had my first love affair with a little mulatta, who was a fine piece of work, Jeremias left me the room and I discovered what making love was all about. Then I lost interest. About that time, Pascualito took me to the sanctuary in Guanabacoa to see the virgin. She was a very pretty virgin, surrounded by flowers. I asked her blessing half-heartedly. I wasn't convinced that a blind girl could cure a cross-eyed guy. Pascualito argued that the painter who did her portrait was drunk and drew her with no eyes. She was really the Virgin of Toledo. When she discovered her condition, she decided to make miracles.

Let me pause to say a few words about Jeremias. He was a tricky fox when it came to women. There wasn't a pretty woman along the Prado Jeremias didn't get into his bed. He was a flashy dresser: flannel hat, loud pants, and two-toned shoes he never parted with. His gruff character was just a front. He also took me to see the city skyline that changed constantly as old buildings crumbled. "Behold Havana, the transvestite," he'd say. "One city today, another city tomorrow. Just like the god, Chango . . ."

With Pascualito the Good, we kept up a familiar dialogue. The dwarf never expressed his opinion about that world of waste water. Only by letting things unfold did I grasp his secrets. He was not at all willing to describe the changes in the Congregation's hierarchy, even less willing to describe the Supreme Boss's misfortunes. I also learned that no dwarf could be buried in the underground. They had ruled out having a cemetery in the cave's vaults and so the dwarves had taken one over in Guanabacoa, abandoned by the Jews who'd fled to New York in the sixties. There I got lucky when Pascualito bestowed upon us the job of digging a grave.

"Tomorrow you and Jeremias will dig the final resting place of a brother who's died," he said.

Cemeteries had always terrified me. We entered the cemetery seized with fear, Jeremias muttering angrily. It was on a small hill, covered with ceiba trees, surrounded by crumbling walls. The Jewish graves were lost among the fallen leaves and you could only identify them by the columns with Hebrew characters. At last we came to the small mounds, next to the adobe wall in the back, where dwarves were buried. That's where we dug and by noon we'd made a small hole. Then, Pascualito appeared alongside the wall and offered us a swallow of a concoction made from some roots. He said he'd give the order to begin the mourners' send-off. When that started he said we'd have to leave since the ceremony was only for residents of the underground. We took our time gathering up our tools and glimpsed the court of the Grail enter, with a great chalice in front held high by a boy dwarf. For the first and only time, I saw the Supreme Boss—"art among arts, guide and splendor, sovereign of the sun," the boy proclaimed. The Supreme Boss was fat, pot-bellied and bare-chested, with a belly button like a tomato. That's as much as we saw because Pascualito shooed us away.

The next week I was promoted to a special delivery service for the sale of household goods. Tulle, flowers, good champagne—the underground had it all. That's when Rosendo Gil came into my life. He ran a laundromat he'd set up in his home on Murral Street. There was a sign at the entrance "Lightning Laundry: Washed and Dried in a Flash." Every day Rosendo handed me a list of deliveries. I don't think I'll ever work that hard again. He handed me deliveries packed with lace outfits and there I was, traveling by bus all the way to the ritzy neighborhoods of Miramar and New Vedado. I saw so many pretty girls undeterred by the bad weather! What I didn't like was those grand homes with gardens and dogs. People there looked at me like I was a criminal. I didn't wear my glasses just to fuck with them. When I rang one of those doorbells in Avon Llama, just like the homes in the commercials, I made myself more cross-eyed.

"You're weird," Rosendo Gil would say to me.

So that's how things went for me in this part of Havana, cut off from my friend Jeremias. Although we shared the room in the Packard, our jobs were so different we hardly ever saw each other. Until my fairy godmother—or bad luck—came along. It was a Wednesday, the 25th of December, my second Christmas in Havana. My delivery was bound for Mason and San Miguel, TV Cubana, ask for Reinita

Principe. I got there and asked for her and they brought her right over. She was the actress who played the maid on the popular soap opera. I had taken off my glasses and my eyes had crossed really hard. At that moment I longed for my eyes to be aligned. The woman said we'll have to wait, Lucecita's taping. You know, my daughter, Lucecita, she clarified.

"I want her to try the outfit on. Then we'll settle up."

Next she invited me to the studio and I saw a TV show for the first time. They were filming Snow White. Lucecita was playing the main role. I'd never, ever seen a girl like her. I've never seen such pretty eyes since. Flung there on a rock, Lucecita was radiant, happiness personified. It was the scene where the Prince saves Snow White, when he arrives and kisses her and she comes back to life. Then, the dwarves dance and run around the studio. The end of the story made me break out in tears.

"This's the guy who brought the ball gown," Lucecita's mother introduced me. I held the box out to her and she smiled with that happy glow and went to try on the outfit. I waited there in limbo, watching the cameras that memorized dreams.

"Doesn't she look lovely!" Reinita Principe said when her daughter returned. The dwarves sang her praises, touching the tulle. All the studio admired her. "Let's go home," her mother urged.

Right now I don't know, I can't figure out if they hoodwinked me into loving her or if I got on board all on my own. They didn't invite me in that day and left me standing outside the door. As we turned the corner at Mason and San Miguel, next to the Napoleonic Museum, across from the university, Reinita Principe said, in the maid's voice she uses in the soap opera, that she had only half the money. She went on about how the TV station was a hell hole, how they weren't doing any shows now that her beauty was fading. And in that situation I wasn't going to back down. I never say too much. I was a businessman, but I didn't know if the dwarves dreamed up everything that went on in Havana. I reasoned to myself, if they were already in TV, they could be anywhere.

"I can give you credit," it occurred to me to say.

"Hey, he's my kind of guy!" said Lucecita.

From that moment on, I believed a woman can change your life with a single word. I became Lucecita's biggest fan. Not an afternoon went by when I wasn't in the studios. I finagled a special pass and sat in the front row, watching the shows. "Is this love?!" I asked myself.

I was hurt when they didn't invite me to Lucecita's birthday party. That night I walked along the University walls. When I saw the fuss they were making over her, I lost the nerve to go in. I remember I went into the Napoleon Museum and stood in front of the Great

Corsican's bed for an hour. I was so smitten by Josephine's portrait, I longed to take it home, just to have a girlfriend. But imagination is one thing, life is another.

"Put the squeeze on the mother," Rosendo Gil told me, who'd become my confessor. "Either she gives you her daughter or she pays," he smiled salaciously.

So I approached Reinita Principe. I told her my boss demanded payment from me and, if I didn't get it, they'd retaliate. Her smile dimmed. She mentioned the money owed her and that she'd been chosen for a leading part. I turned a deaf ear and spoke of the terrible band of thieves that lurk around houses at night. She promised she'd take care of the debt that very week. Transformed from then on, she scolded me for not coming to the party. I looked at her with such scorn she changed the subject and invited me over for coffee.

"I want you to meet my husband," she said.

It was a typical Havana apartment that had seen better days: furniture missing its upholstery, crumbling walls, broken windows. Reinita tiptoed in and said, "Nicanor Jose." All we heard was a rasping cough. Reinita said, "Follow me," and we entered a bedroom where a man in his seventies was smoking a cigar. Behind him, tacked to the wall, were photos, posters, diplomas, and a map of Havana. The main photo—for some reason I guessed the caption was in German—must have said something banned. It showed a crane setting a concrete block down in the middle of a street. At the street's end, there was a trolley that had come to a stop. Lucecita's old man was barefoot, wearing a sweater that hung down over his wool pants. He looked me over and, seeing my interest in the photo, said it was the all-powerful Berlin Wall.

"It was the wall that saved us," he said. Then he showed me his diplomas, describing them like in a newsreel at the movie theater. "Ah, this one! From the KGB, a year-long course in Moscow. Oh, this one, from that second rate Czech security agency! Yes, that one, from the highly trained German police force!" He coughed again and spit out the window, then pointed to the map of Havana. "See those circles? See them?" he asked, forcing me to answer yes quickly. "That's where the sewers empty out. I was the one who discovered the scourge, I was the first to say the city was being taken over by the Jews who disappeared from the synagogues in Havana just as the Berlin Wall was being built. They hid underground and became predators, draining the people dry."

From then on, I became a regular visitor. Reinita Principe told me her husband had been an officer and had traveled all over the world taking courses in espionage. They'd discharged him when he raised a ruckus at a meeting with the generals, insisting, to no avail, that there were dwarves in the sewers of Havana.

"Then came the fall of the Wall," Reinita explained. "And he hasn't gotten over it. Every waking moment, he has cursed Vaclav Havel. He once met him in Prague, you know."

Lucecita didn't like the fact that I visited every day, loaded down with cans of sausages. Her mother pressured her to be polite but Lucecita took great pains to sour my life. For the whole month I stayed for supper, she sat at the table and stared at me or made comments about people who thought they could buy love. I doted on her, tried to flatter her more each day and spent my savings generously. But she didn't repay my generosity. She persuaded her father to declare war on me. The old man began his campaign against me and threatened to have his old comrades arrest me as a Jewish spy.

"Make yourself scarce," my friend Jeremias advised me.

That's what I did. I didn't set foot in the studio or the house. Such sadness came over me! I had no desire to spite her by sleeping with one of those girls for hire. I started to hate Havana and my memories. In the afternoons I went to the Dos Hermanos Bar and got really drunk. There were the same longshoremen, the Chinese mulatta who squeezed me dry that night by the light of El Morro. Everyone kept touching my head.

A month later my life took a new turn. One afternoon I ran across Pascualito at the entrance to the Packard. The little guy beckoned to me to follow him. He talked about the Great Grail, the Supreme Boss and the difficulties they had picking up the TV signal underground. He asked me if I was still catting around in the studios at Mason and San Miguel. When I explained my amorous setbacks, he insisted I go back to the studio and focus all my time on spying.

"They'll pay you well."

"Why me? What about those mountebank dwarves?"

"Oh, no, they're artists."

I went back to Mason and San Miguel and got in Reinita Principe's good graces. I made friends with producers, set designers, cameramen. In two weeks I managed to make off with building plans and a list of guards. I had a clear picture of how the studio was run. Because her mother forced her to, Lucecita began to flirt with me and insisted I visit their home again.

In the blink of an eye, I resumed my visits, loaded down with provisions. They locked the old man up in his room and Reinita lit incense and we got drunk. Lucecita drank too much and was toasting the birdies circling her head, like in the cartoons. At exactly midnight, we uncorked some hard cider and Reinita pushed me toward her daughter's bedroom. Lucecita was still talking to the birdies and I stammered in fear as if I'd smoked pot. She asked me never to take off my glasses. "You're cuter that way." And I fell asleep by her side, peaceful, barely touching her.

"It's our secret," she conspired with me.

That morning, in a spectacular raid that took Havana by surprise, the studio at Mason and San Miguel was dismantled. From Reinita herself I learned they'd caught the night guards sleeping on the job. She also told me there'd be an investigation and they'd dredge up Havana as if it were a mined field.

"There's a lot of hatred," she said.

And me? They simply forgot about me. They even interviewed the street sweepers and no one remembered me. I didn't exist.

"I'm invisible," I told Lucecita.

"Cheer up," she answered. "That may be the very thing I'll love about you some day."

Pascualito met up with me at Rosendo Gil's home and said that the Great Grail sent their congratulations. The Supreme Boss would give me a medal and I could ask for anything I wanted. I didn't know what to say. It was Pascualito who suggested a restaurant.

"What do I have to do?" I asked.

"Nothing. Live and look after the Grail's share."

It was easy to convince Lucecita to set up the restaurant in her home. People worked hard in those days. From out of the sewers came the tables, tablecloths, food, everything. My good friend Jeremias was the supplier for our new business. That was the only condition I'd set. He became someone who handed out happiness. The same sort of thing happened to Reinita Principe, and I asked myself if Jeremias had won the heart of that pitiful actress. What's more, Lucecita came to love me. I don't know if she loved me out of pity or because of the money we were making. But I swear, one night, she told me I should stop acting like a silly fool. I made such love to her that the sun found us still in bed. For a short time after that, I was the hardest working guy in town.

My restaurant was always full, open twenty-four hours, decorated with posters from the country's heroic days. There's nothing a foreigner likes more than bygone heroism. You should see how they went crazy over a worker's fist held high or the gears of a machine flattening bureaucracy. Lucecita's father got in on the act, too. Tourists gathered in his room and he recreated the story of his travels through KGB headquarters and the afternoon he saw Vaclav Havel in the middle of a Prague snowstorm. The old man recounted his biography with pride, donning his old military jacket and displaying the map of Havana and repeating his story about the conspiracy. Although he never thought to charge, each day Reinita left a five dollar bill in a silver ashtray to give the visitors the idea.

About that same time, my mother died. I had her frozen and brought from our town and gave her a Christian burial with bundles of aspirin and cough syrup alongside her in one of the niches at the

Falla Bonet Cemetery. My mother never dreamed she'd be laid to rest on Carrara marble. During that time, Lucecita and I got married in the church. It was a sumptuous wedding. I was decked out in a black suit and a turquoise tie. Five months later Pascual Jeremias was born, named for my two friends.

"You're a winner!" my mother told me in a letter shortly before her death. I felt so proud I forgot I was cross-eyed, I forgot all about my suffering, the injustices. I was starting to see life as one endless spending spree. There was no one at the door of my heart to give me a wake up call. About that time laziness caught up with me. Little by little Lucecita took over the reins of the business. She knew how to juggle the day's sales figures and she carefully divided the Grail's money, money for the inspectors, bribes to keep them quiet and of course some money for us.

"That extra money will make us rich," she said one night.

"What if they find out?" I said fearfully.

"How will they know?" she said kissing my waist and taking off my glasses for the first time. "Who's going to talk? You? Me? Jeremias?"

Now I know that part of life's adventure is taking big risks. Good fortune went out with the old man and the toilet bowl. See, we made sure he didn't talk. But the old guy still found a way to communicate, to get the word out. He scrounged every mayonnaise jar, every mustard jar, filled them with letters telling all about our evil deeds and put them in circulation with every flush of the toilet.

The first fateful sign came the Monday Jeremias disappeared. I tried in vain to find him. I went to the Packard, searched his room, peered into every corner of the Prado where he made his conquests. No one had seen him since Friday. Then I visited Pascualito at his spot in front of the train station. I tried to hug him and he pulled away from me. He spoke of the cruel moon that poisons the human heart. He told of the waters that wash you clean of shame.

"Something funny's going on," I told Lucecita when I got back.

"Jeremias is in love and Pascualito's a neurotic dwarf," she said, trying to calm me down.

"The dark age is coming," I said.

"No! Our son won't be forced to do the same jobs we had to do," Lucecita answered.

"The dark age is coming," I said.

And I was right. At dawn a horde of dwarves attacked us. In minutes they cleaned out everything. A big-breasted female dwarf snatched Pascual Jeremias from his cradle. Then they carried off Lucecita and Reinita Principe. The old man disappeared, wrapped up in his map of Havana. I stood there without the strength or will to act. At that moment, Pascualito walked in and repeated that line about the cruel moon and signaled for them to carry me off. He kissed me on the cheek and I don't remember anything after that.

I awoke in an ice storeroom in a cavern. My body was trembling. Good Jeremias came toward me. Oh, my God! He was a despicable dwarf! Short legs, an old double-breasted coat over his small body, his ears mangled, wearing felt boots, not his two-toned shoes. He had an air of resignation that horrified me.

"I don't exist any more," he told me, helping me to my feet. That was when my cry froze the cavern even more. I was a dwarf, too, a dwarf with lips tangled up by confusion, a dwarf with no eyelashes.

"You'll get used to it," he declared like a priest who'd talked on and on about Christ's commandments, about punishment and absolution. He spoke Pontius Pilate's name as if he were a patron saint of that winter. "How long will I be like this?" I sobbed.

"For eternity," was his reply.

Today there was a slaughter. The slaughterhouse is next to this freezer and, since dawn, all throughout the day's work, the cows' moos have tormented me. I wonder if the cows ponder life and death. But those subtleties are moot. My tragedy is double: I've stopped breathing the air of Havana and I'm despised. Dwarves—I talk as if I weren't one—have a definite standard of beauty. They're delighted with their short bodies and beautiful eyes, a trait of their brotherhood. For that reason I have to do the worst jobs. Tote boxes, cut out the cows' livers, cremate their bones, slice off the bulls' tongues.

"The Big Show's about to start," Jeremias tells me, still my faithful friend. Now I'll end my story. Now I'll sit in front of the TV—the only pastime allowed—and come face to face with Lucecita. Artists always manage to weasel out of their punishment. It's a program made for her on underground TV. They'll introduce her as the World Famous Vedette from the Follies Bergere. She'll come on with all the under-appreciated sensuality she's capable of displaying. A human sized Lucecita for the lonely nights of my torment. Every time I see her, I forget about that normal-sized woman, the lover I adored. All I care about is whether my Pascual Jeremias was saved like his mother. Now Jeremias calls to me that the show's starting. I'd give the world to stop hearing that Glenn Miller tune broadcast over and over on the loud speakers. I want to have wings and fly, take my son with me like the jaguars from the legends and climb that mountain that is Havana and, there, be a man. My Lucecita sings the show's theme song and I travel across that space of light and fantasy on the screen to love her.

Translation by Pamela Carmell

The Happy Death of Alborada Almanza

Leonardo Padura Fuentes

Alborada Almanza woke up gently but completely, with the keen sensation that something extraordinary was going to happen to her that day. She had barely opened her eyes when she felt the sharp prick of premonition, and she tried to figure out the cause. It was a seizure of joy after another bad night plagued, like always, with intense nightmares in colors that she couldn't remember. From her bed she observed the calendar, the one she had made herself, and although today was the saint's day of her beloved Saint Raphael the Archangel, the date did not appear to suggest anything special because it wasn't her birthday, or any other birthday she could remember, and it wasn't the long awaited day on which groceries would be sent from the corner *bodega*.

Slowly, so as not to aggravate the stiffness of her arthritis, Alborada slipped her feet out of the bed and into a pair of threadbare slippers. Summoning all of her strength, she got out of bed and stood perfectly upright all at once. That was when she began to fear that the beautiful beginning of the day was just another dirty trick of her nightmares: the very thing that made her endure hunger, heat and old age. But for the moment, everything was light and pleasing, very much like a vigil. I must be sure to enjoy a dream like this, she thought. She felt a surge of confidence that the day might bring something unexpected, even if it weren't her birthday or the day when groceries would arrive. She walked to the kitchen with a determined air and checked the jar where she kept coffee, searching for the incontrovertible evidence that she was in a dream. The smell of rich dark coffee that filled the jar made her happy. How different from the customary and tormenting absence of coffee; the allotment of a meager two ounces of coffee every two weeks barely lasted for three breakfasts, and for the remaining twelve days the morning grumbling of her intestines had to be satisfied with concoctions of anise, orange leaves, or bits of soursop, prepared with a plentiful dose of sugar to stir up energy and fortify her for another day.

While the water for coffee was heating, Alborada searched the cupboard for the packet of powdered cereal, the kind with a soil aftertaste and astringent qualities, that served as breakfast on many a morning. To her delight, she saw, intact and triumphant, a can of condensed milk with two cows on the label and the familiar Russian letters. It had been ten years since that thick and creamy milk had disappeared from the Island's markets, yet there it was.

And that milk would have been the best gift possible except that on the stove top, near where the water and coffee were coming to a boil, Alborada discovered two flaky pastries filled with guava paste, the kind that her husband, Tobias, used to bring her every morning from 1933 to 1967. The pastries stopped when the neighborhood bakery was shut down by a committee of the Revolution. And along with them, gone forever, were the chocolate *montecristos*, the coconut *masarreals* and the petite Morón cakes.

It's worthwhile to dream after all, mused Alborada as she strained the coffee. Its rich and invigorating aroma—strong enough to awaken the dead—filled the air. "What if it wakes me up?" she thought with alarm. She decided to devour the two pastries first, drink the condensed milk, and then slowly savor the perfectly measured coffee. Since it followed the pastries and the sweet milk, it tasted just a little more bitter than usual. Fearfully, Alborada sipped the coffee and waited for the dreadful awakening, the eternal aching in her bones and the rumbling dissatisfaction of her bowels. She even closed her eyes to make everything seem more natural, but when she discovered that the taste of coffee lingered in her mouth, she understood wondrously that it would not be easy to take leave of such an exotic and absurd dream.

Following the command of her skin, Alborada took off her clothes in the kitchen. She let the worn nightgown that had lost all its lace fall on a chair; she undid the string that held up her drooping underpants—a loose fit over the bones of her hips—and allowed them to drop to the floor. Although she was having the best dream of her life, everything seemed so real that Alborada preferred not to run the risk of seeing her body wasted by the privations and hunger of the last few years. She walked toward the shower, head held high, with the anticipation of bathing with Palmolive soap, brushing her false teeth with her favorite brand of toothpaste, and applying a perfumed Avon lotion that she had seen for the last time when it was a gift for her forty-eighth birthday in 1962.

As the water purified her and the Palmolive soap caressed her body, Alborada had the feeling that she was not alone. It was a remote sensation, like all those she was receiving this morning, because not since the death of Tobias, twenty-two years ago, had anyone shared the bathroom with her.

"How nice it is not to be alone," she said out loud, because the sensation that someone was with her was as palpable as each of the small pleasures that had been rescued from forgotten times, like the agility that was returning to her flaccid muscles, like the desire to never wake up and to live forever in that world where guava pastries, condensed milk, Palmolive soap, and above all coffee—pure coffee, without horrifying extenders—were as common as was their absence in the world where she had been living. There, in the harsh contours of her real life, she'd gone to bed hungry at night more than once and when she looked up through the cracks in the roof at the star-filled sky, she had asked God and Saint Raphael the Archangel to grant her a quick and painless death that would free her from the nightmares, the heat, and the morning infusions doused with sugar.

"That's why I'm here," said the presence. Alborada thought about covering up but something stopped her. "I'm glad you smell so good . . ."

"Is it you?" asked the elderly woman.

"Who else could it be? I am Raphael, one of the seven archangels in the Lord's service, one of those allowed to abide in his glorious presence. You asked for me to come and the Lord has granted your request."

"Then . . .?"

"Yes, Alborada, you are dead just as you wished, and I have come for you. Put on your perfume because we are going to heaven."

"Oh my goodness," murmured the woman, contemplating the loss of what she had only very recently recovered.

"What's the matter? Why do you doubt?"

Alborada pushed back the shower curtain and saw before her a tall, strong, luminous mulatto completely nude and without the wings he was supposed to have. Between his legs shone a brilliant penis furrowed with purple veins and with the glans red and polished, like the apples Alborada used to offer to her beloved Saint Barbara.

"You don't look like him . . ." she said, unable to take her eyes off of his magnificent member and pointing toward the rosy sphinx that she had in the room.

"You should really say that he doesn't look like me. Is it that you don't like me the way I am?"

"No, it's not that. It's that you're so human. And, well, to have to leave right now, like this . . ."

"That's what you asked for. On my day, the Lord allows me to choose the person I want to take with me, and the way in which the person is taken. Since you are practically a saint, I decided to grant your wish."

"But when I wanted to die I didn't have coffee, or pastries, or milk . . . and now that I have tasted them again . . ."

"You want to stay for things like that? To abandon heaven and be condemned to hell?"

Alborada began to tremble. Now she knew she was dead and it didn't matter because the suffering and deprivations of her life would never return. The terrible part was that the ritual coffee mixture—a sorry excuse for the real thing—that she drank six times a month, the scent of sweet basil with which she seasoned her meals, and the expectation of finding out who the heroine of the soap opera would marry would not return either. Life could be terrible, but it was life.

"Yes, Alborada, you are dead and you are going to heaven."

"And, if I don't want to?" she dared to ask. Nothing worse could befall her now. Suddenly she realized that the entire bizarre dialogue carried out while she was totally nude, made her feel uninhibited and freed from the sense of fear she had known her entire life. It is really awful that this is happening to me when I'm dead, she thought.

"I'm sorry," said the Archangel, smiling for the first time. "That's the way life is. Some go to heaven for being brave, and others for being cowards. There's no turning back now. I am the reward for your fear . . ."

"Thanks for your sincerity . . ." murmured the elderly woman who had recently died.

At last she dared to look at her body: it was old, wrinkled, with bones right near the surface of the skin: a bad reminder of her other existence, a malignant proof that some miracles never occur. Then she understood that it was best to simply obey, like she'd always done. After all, she already knew what hell was like and perhaps in heaven there would be guava pastries and coffee: the coffee that she remembered longing for when she was still alive and used to cast forlorn glances at the gloomy and almost-bare pantry.

"Are there pastries in heaven?"

"Always, and freshly baked. That's why it's called Glory."

"All right . . . Can I do something else before we leave?"

"That depends, Alborada," whispered the Archangel.

"It's very simple: I want to see the ocean, I want to pet a dog, and I want to hear a *danzón.*"

The celestial mulatto smiled again and Alborada felt her cheeks blush.

"Granted," he said. "On the condition that you let me dance the *danzón* with you. It's been centuries since I danced."

"It will be an honor," said Alborada looking at the spectacular attribute of the mulatto sent from heaven. She thought for a moment and concluded that her cowardice had been worth the price: at long last she was going to a place where they served warm guava pastries. God had given her the best of all possible deaths, and she was going to heaven to the rhythm of "Almendra," her favorite *danzón.*

Translation by Anne Fountain

Waters

Alejandro Aguilar

The last trip from the gas station had left him thoroughly exhausted. The distance, the weight, the climb up the steep staircase, all had conspired to crush him. Now before his eyes, defying his famished body, is the rusty container with the hostile red ink letters, DRINKING WATER, written in a thick scrawl, the leg of the A extending like a mocking tongue. He lowers himself to the floor, barely keeping his balance. Crouching barefoot, he flinches at the contrast in temperature between his overheated muscles, his sweaty skin, and his testicles as they graze the cold and grimy floor tiles. He attempts to stand up but fatigue overwhelms him. He ponders the hours spent without a single bite of food, and the greenish mildew staining the bathroom walls with whimsical splotches. He watches the sunlight filter in through crooked blinds and spread around the room until there is scarcely enough light to make out the letters on the container. His legs twitch and he needs to piss. He tries to get back on his feet again, succeeds this time, and starts to move around. The faded piece of shirt he uses for soap is all too familiar. Months ago the harshness of the fabric and the seams bruised his skin, but now he rubs vigorously, even happily. The treated water gets him to imagining that he's a luxury automobile in an automatic carwash. Such thoughts use up the last bit of humor he had deliberately saved for Sunday.

In the kitchen, still standing, he gulps down two spoonfuls of soggy rice and peas, those same *petit pois* that could be so good when mixed with a little cream à la St. Germain. But with neither electricity nor spices, there is no way to dress up these basic, cold, salt-free little green balls to boot. He feels a stab of pain in his stomach and the fine mesh protecting his brain begins to unravel. There is a universal remedy for headache—aspirin—but he will have to make do with a sea breeze. His neighbor systematically refuses to give him any medicine, driven by a mean habit of hoarding or, more accurately, by her fanatical guarding of strategic reserves.

Immersed in his worries, he steps out onto the street. Crossing a cave-dark intersection, he is almost run over by a barely visible bicycle. The scream, "Are you blind, you sonofabitch?" sounds too metallic to be coming from a human being. He is overwhelmed by the suspicion that the machine has somehow managed to go riderless, and talk.

At length the sea breeze on his face wipes away the bad mood and

those absurd thoughts as if they were dust. His headache subsides
with the sound of the waves prancing over the reefs, oblivious to the
dangers of being ripped apart by the coral's sharp edges. Hordes of
people walk by him going in the opposite direction: youngsters bent
on weird exploits; adults chasing after the unknown even as they
hawk the most exotic items; resplendent half-naked young women
showing off their bodies and offering their company to anyone who
looks foreign. Other gray silhouettes, seemingly lost in their mute-
ness, sway in the soft evening wind. And, occasionally, the dull
motor of some ancient car or the hiss of a tourist minivan calls to
mind a witches' Sabbath, a gathering of early-rising predators and
lewd black women. The rest is shadows and the ceaseless splashing
of waves.

He searches for a suitable place on the seawall, away from noisy
groups and necking couples. On a concrete jetty, a man hunches
silently, alone and folded into himself. This is not really the kind of
atmosphere he is looking for, but, out of respect for the other man,
he asks if it is OK for him to sit there and if he can help. A shrug
is the only answer. He settles down with some difficulty, trying to
find the serenity he craves. But it is not easy. The day loaded with
incidents, the humidity seeping through the worn fabric of his pants,
and the ever-present sea, dark and brooding, water everywhere,
barely covered by dirt-covered roads pulsating with chaotic lives.
That is all, an island and the certainty of the city with its random
sounds. Far away, closer to the horizon than to the tips of his toes, a
swarm of colored lights signals the passage of a garish cruise ship,
its otherworldliness deepened by the distance. The shape to his right
clings to the edge of the seawall and leans over the water, vomiting
with spasms and noises that make him fear the body will just spill
out, abandon the wrinkled skin, and float up above the city, like
scraps of paper in a gathering storm. Minutes later, and somewhat
recovered, the figure casts out an orphaned question, seemingly as
preamble to a suicide. The little man stares at him for the first time,
and, unable to keep his balance, waivers between looking at the
intruder and out to sea, where his glance finally comes to rest. "Can
I do anything for you?" He tries to gain time, gets ready to help, but
the other man's broken voice takes up a litany, a mixture of curses
with bits and pieces of an unintelligible story, speaking to the whole
city and to no one in particular. Who would answer?

His attempt to get out of himself has failed. He decides to amble
toward the big hotels but something catches his eye. A dark woman,
tall yet fragile, and a very pale and blonde woman are exchanging
a black baby, while splitting some wrinkled bills they were carrying
in their bosom. He catches the drift and concludes that imagination knows no bounds. Looking at the occasional mothers with their

rented baby, he is convinced he was not delirious when he thought the bicycle was riderless and could speak.

He decides to return home, has every intention of lying down to rest. But he is still not used to sleeping alone. His wife left him a few days ago without a word of explanation—not that he demanded any—just when he was about to admit to himself that he had become indifferent to her presence. She had turned into a shadow hovering over his daily concerns, a noise that distracted him from the tricks he had developed to make it alive to the end of every day. Actually, it was lucky that she had made such a quiet exit, like the French are known to do.

The power is out and God treats him to a long and particularly scorching sleepless night. Shortly before dawn, a divine perk. A few feet away from his eyes, in the room across the street, a woman walks around naked and vulnerable in front of an open window in shimmering candlelight. Her body glistens with sweat and the most beautiful insomnia he has ever witnessed. Lust turns him into a hormone-crazed adolescent who lets up only when his legs are about to buckle. Is it hunger or pleasure? He will never know. No matter. It is one fine way to start the day.

Elbows resting on the remains of a park bench, he becomes absorbed in the unfolding morning. The splendid sun in the usual flawlessly blue sky. The day premiering with the bustle of people going places, of kids waiting for their school friends, of shriveled old people straining to be at the head of the endless shortage lines. How beautiful the city is as it awakens! Some young dude from the barrio walks by and, sensing his moroseness, offers him a swig to gladden his day. And also to challenge the old ladies who, out of sheer inertia, adamantly try to control everything that goes on around them. As he walks away the youngster yells, Yeah, a swig feels good this time of day. Hey, it's already night in Europe and their bars and discotheques are hopping, so long live geography! That next to the last swig hits him squarely in the neck, the eyes, and especially the stomach. His eyes mist over, setting aquiver the monument to the last mayor of the city to be freely elected, sometime around the beginning of the century. The statue, in the middle of the park, dims and seems to lower an arm weary from holding up his steel saber. He gets up to clear his head knowing that, in the absence of a cold shower, walking is a possible cure. Besides, that way he can discover new corners of this withered city each day: a crack here, a collapsed wall there, foul-smelling puddles, hydrants oozing blackened waters.

He strolls aimlessly around and, unwittingly, makes his way back to the gas station. The guard recognizes him. We're really in bad shape today, citizen. Citizen. How long had it been since he had heard that word? Got any gas? he tries to fake it. No gas, no oil, no air. Plus the drinking water ran out last night. People even carried off the tank, so go ahead and keep the can I lent you yesterday since I won't be needing it anytime soon. The guard, all his years heavy with silence, tips back his stool, and stares at him wondering what will become of the old man in that gutted building.

He has almost finished the third bottle of homemade rum that tastes like sheer heaven to him. The image of the empty can breaks through his mind's fog. It sits uselessly on the grimy bathroom tiles, those red letters dancing mockingly in the twilight.

DRINKING WATER   DRINKING WATER   DRINKING WATER

By now it is close to six, and he has wandered back to the same piece of bench. Fatigued and nauseous he lies down on the grass, all the while staring at the clouds, at the stubbornly blue sky that denies the gift of a shower. There is no hint of rain, no threat of storm. Up there, in the distance, there is a tiny silver speck. He asks himself for the umpteenth time where airplanes go, what one feels inside that bird-like machine, what he would do if he ever got to board one. And then he thinks he might just pass the time looking down trying to spot, between one body of water and the next, those guys who lie down in parks to watch the clouds and the planes.

Translation by Cristina de la Torre

The Colonel's Allegro

Alejandro Aguilar

David has a colonel for a neighbor, a very nice man. Every morning the colonel greets him as he leaves for work in his spotless uniform and sunglasses, always admiring the shine of his own shoes. It is unusual to see a person nearing sixty come down the stairs so nimbly. Even more unusual is to hear him say *"Buenos días"* without so much as looking up. That is one of the colonel's unusual habits, David has noticed, but so what, he still greets him faithfully as he leaves for work—just when David is returning from his nightly jaunts. David answers with a somewhat tentative *"Buenos días"* uttered sideways so as to reach its mark on the rebound, in the hope that his alcoholic breath will cling to the walls and avoid the range of the colonel's nose, which rests above his thick mustache and under his dark glasses. It never quite works, and when their paths cross, as David is on the way up and the colonel is going down to his car—where the chauffeur (or whatever the military term is for the person who drives the colonel's car, who is the same person who lugs the shopping bags of the colonel's wife, who comes in and out carrying either empty or full gasoline cans, bottles of rum and cases of beer, who shines the car, and stops by with his wife occasionally to pay a social call on Mr. & Mrs. Colonel) is waiting—David has noticed that the colonel turns his torso ever so slightly to continue looking him up and down so accusingly that he feels a weight on his back that makes it hard for him to climb the steps. But if the colonel is thinking something horrible, it must not be that horrible because he keeps it to himself. Or he used to.

A few days ago the nice colonel crossed paths with David, like most mornings, on the stairs. David and Tom. David greeted him with the usual *"Buenos días,"* only this time it was projected towards the ceiling to avoid seeing himself reflected on the colonel's dark glasses. And the colonel started to reciprocate with his usual greeting, his eyes fixed, as usual, on the shine of his own shoes. The routine was unfolding in its usual awkward way when, suddenly, everything froze and not just due to silence. Tom, who uttering a "Hello," changed the peaceful course of the encounter, sustained with difficulty until then, so that in one second, or perhaps even less, the sparkle of the colonel's dark glasses abandoned the shine of his shoes, climbed diagonally up the wall and came to a standstill on the limpid eyes and unmistakably American face of the youth. Tom's presence loomed. And never before had the silence of a withheld greeting sounded so much like the cannon shots that signal the opening of hostilities in war. David's nice colonel neighbor halted the passage of time, the motion of air and sound in one single look and, from that moment on, nothing would ever be the same, not even the sober greetings exchanged each morning as they met on the stairs when the colonel left for his duties and David returned from his nightly forays. What was it that altered the precarious balance, the subdued tension, the violence so far suppressed thanks to the wholesome habit of the reticent greeting? It was Tom's American accent. That "Hello" that should never have been uttered. The enemy's flagrant presence was seeping into zones already threatened by David's existence: someone much too effeminate for the taste of the colonel's other neighbors, much too cool, wild, and irresponsible, for the colonel's own. But David was a homegrown product. How to put it? A sicko, a pervert, yes, but nevertheless someone perfectly controllable, limitable, repressible, disappearable even, in the closed circuit of the building, the neighborhood, the country, the nation. The homeland! But how to accept, admit, tolerate, apprehend, reduce, oppress, destroy, erase, an alien arrived precisely from there, from that region of the planet whose image had been, for the colonel, nothing less than the bull's-eye of the target on which all his regiment's weapons had been trained, on which all the efforts of the men, who obeyed the slightest sparkle of his dark glasses, were focused? MEN, yes, straight, hard men, tempered by the ennobling endeavor of bearing arms in the service of their country: men. Single-minded, inscrutable men, untarnished, imperturbable. Everything around David's nice colonel neighbor had to be an extension of the untainted quality of his regiment; everything except for David, that inconsequential, insignificant pervert, tolerable as a neighbor. How long had his licentious ways been allowed, his coming home to sleep off the damage done by his shameless orgies just at the moment when the colonel, and all the other upstanding neighbors, were leaving for work? Much too long. And the proof was right there. In that muscled, rosy cheeked, insolent, aggressively handsome boy whose apparition tore through the dark surface of the colonel's glasses thanks to a strategy that he knew only too well: surprise. Just as it had been conceived in order to compensate for an enemy's numerical superiority, used to wrench away the initiative and control him, the strategy of surprise played a role in this encounter. Under the dark cover of his impenetrable glasses, the colonel blinked. He stumbled slightly, briefly lost his balance and, for the first time ever, had to reach for the railing in order to turn his torso and admire that boy escaped from enemy lines, that flawless gringo, as flawless as the majority of his men who, when standing erect swelled their chests out, tightened their buttocks and, as a result, the bulge between their legs became more evident than ever. And, as the colonel reviewed his troops one by one, his face before each of theirs, his eyes, hidden behind the dark curtain of his glasses, would plunge straight down to those succulent bulges that now accompanied the gallant stance, the aggressive, charging stance of his soldiers, untainted, unpolluted, invincible, untouchable. Once David's nice colonel neighbor reached the street and the curving stairs blocked the vision of the two gorgeous guys cheerfully climbing, he let out a sigh. The rays of the morning sun blinded him momentarily, intensifying the arousal that still unnerved him. Once again he breathed deeply, regaining his composure, and headed for the car where the person who drives, carries things in and out, comes and goes, where that who-knows-what-he-is-called-in-military-speak person was waiting. The colonel settled stiffly into his seat and, staring straight ahead, gave orders to proceed to headquarters. While he went over in his mind the things on that day's agenda, his imagination fluttered toward those bodies just admired on the stairs, and, like every morning, the colonel let his hand rest languidly on the inviting and well-padded bulge on the soldier's crotch, the same one who drives, carries things in and out, comes and goes, and no one knows what to call him when things like these go on between David's nice colonel neighbor and one of his own regiment's unpolluted soldiers. Just then, David opened the door to his place and, softly pressing his hand on Tom's hip, invited him in.

Translation by Cristina de la Torre

A Nude in the Rain

Ena Lucía Portela

For Evelyn Hatch, should she ever come
back to life

One rainy afternoon, E settles down in front of the camera. A powder flash (so to speak) in the studio's shadows and, *voilà*: for the umpteenth time, Bruno captures her smile.

E's smile. I'll repeat that phrase many times, in many ways; that look on her face, imprecise, not in time or space, but in the vast number of things you can read into it—an unclear, ironic expression, you might say. Stubbornly natural. You could even polish it up and keep it in a little ivory or marble box, on a whatnot shelf along with other curios from bygone eras. But that wouldn't do any good.

The enclosed space and time of day have no bearing on the deep twilight in Bruno's studio. He set it up, it's artificial, to duplicate an intimate atmosphere, late afternoon, so sultry it makes your head swim, but you stay on your feet thanks to a small dose of amphetamines. In it (the twilight), the soft box mutes the colors and the thin rays of light the lamp casts. The lattice on the window diffuses the outside light into ghostly leopard spots in a ghostly jungle over E's body and the soft surfaces outlining it. The umbrella casts a golden light on an even wider area: E's ambivalent smile, the rain inside . . .

Sounds pretty good: rain inside, her ambivalent smile, the leopard . . . an excellent stage set. A guy could get all romantic and sing along with the victrola-era songs till he's convinced he's the greatest sorcerer in the world, crafter of beautiful phrases for some patient reader to pour over and paradoxes to unravel while stretched out in an easy chair. And that's where things go haywire, where the true message gets sidetracked, fades and takes on the deceitful tint of a phony bleached blond.

Because, Bruno admits, it looks dreadful. Despite all the manifestos and all the scholarly writing and all the semiotic theories about how Botticelli painted his *Birth of Venus*, his *Spring* and other noteworthy canvases culled from the catalog of some long lost art gallery. Despite all that—which wouldn't fit on these few pages and would take volumes and volumes and some prestigious endorsement to give it its proper due—let's not overlook the fact that no description can do a visual image justice. An image either speaks for itself or it's shit.

Bruno has told E that that look won't do, smiling that way spoils everything. He repeated those same words yesterday and Friday, more proof there's a region, a vast region, where the futility of words reigns. If she needs to know why (some girls are really quite smart and Bruno has concluded that E's one of them), he explains that last night he developed some shots from a previous shoot. So, doubting woman, you can go look at them if you like. They're hanging in the basement. Maybe somebody'll like them, some reader in his armchair or E herself, who'd rather see herself as at least spiritual, ethereal, soulful, but they're a real disaster. They're more romantic—or experimental, like photos from the era when photography was an avant-garde art form—than what he's after. They piss him off, make him want to pull his hair out. If the great sorcerer showed them under the title, "How to de-erotify the erotic object," they would be the epitome of what not to do.

What's the problem? Nothing, no matter how much he retouched them, moving shadows and lights from one place to another, toning down the leopard spots, your eye still doesn't go to her nipples, the main thing he wanted to highlight. Inconceivable, since her nipples are big and very erect, as if they were aimed at an invisible enemy lurking on the roof or in the corners of the studio. They embody the desire to pinch them, suck them, bite them . . .

This and this alone is what Bruno's going for: a provocative, playful image, the urge to attack them and caress them at the same time. No airbrushing—he doesn't use any type of filter—or technological innovations. Most of all he wants the essence, what's already invented, the everyday. The eternal. Not an excuse for reflection or pondering. No poetry. Nothing to come between E and the observer's most urgent fantasies. Unfortunately her smile devours all of that. With a force he doesn't quite get, her smile becomes the central focus that devours his objectives.

She shrugs and says well, let's try again. She never questions, never argues, never resists him. She doesn't seem resigned, uncomfortable, tired or even annoyed. She seems to feel absolutely nothing, not even indifference. Aponia, ataraxia, blood thick as a milkshake, the very stereotype of a person who becomes an English aristocrat or a Tibetan monk. Bruno isn't sure she's listening to him. Yet between bursts of light, he senses she's not lying, she's willing to cooperate. Still he's wary of her image on the film.

But sometimes his thoughts get fuzzy, he lets his guard down and a complacent, cheerful demon takes over and he coochie coos her stomach with a feather and makes funny faces—the same thing happens to writers, musicians, artists and other sorcerers—and then, still caught in the vicious cycle, in the *ritornelle*, his critic's eye eludes him and he sees only what he wants to see. A little puppet who puts on a cape to dance, then takes it off again, a whirling griffin, a serpent biting its own tail. To escape that, he would have to quit the game, knock down his king—well protected after the *fianchetto*—and take a walk, witness a traffic accident, someone's arms and legs twitching under a double-long bus, a landslide, a fist fight, have a beer. This woman confuses him.

Like a beginner, he writes it all down: the type of camera (the same kind as always, but no one's hired me to do an ad), the brand and speed of the film (*ibid*), exposure time and lens aperture. All fine. Brazenly fine. The only problem is her smile. But no one can overpower E's smile. If you can, we'll give you an extra large shrimp pizza or a South Seas cruise, absolutely free! Forget Utopias! It (her smile) can win out over any high-tech gadgets, no matter how expensive, and who knows how many photography classes, not counting years of experience. What do I do? Bruno asks himself when a wave of futility washes over him, whenever he feels he's repeating himself.

Thunder rumbles, the rain falls harder, pinging against the windows.

E stretches out on the rug again, surrounded by big cushions, like in a Titian painting. Or in a Manet that, perhaps unconsciously, parodies a Titian: where there was a splay-legged puppy, here there's a muscular cat, its hair standing on end; where there was the Venus of Urbino, here there's Olympia; the backdrop and servant girl are duplicates in the end. Yet neither Venus' majesty nor Olympia's brazenness of the second satisfies our artist. Neither of these women arouses him, God forgive him. Maybe the pose is the problem, he thinks, it's so contrived, like the Duchess of Alba and so many other women painted in oil, water colors or pastels. He motions for E to spread her legs.

He'd wanted to leave that for last. The usual routine: the model covers herself with one hand, reveals more and more, and finally shows with feigned carelessness more than she hides—you know it's fake, you're no dummy. But it's like in the theater: the audience has no qualms about taking part in the fantasy. Her index finger points to a vortex that comes into sharper and sharper focus, as if whispering in your ear "See? See this? How do you like it?", and then a close-up, then another and another, with no fingers and no tricks. Ah, the index finger must be like E's! Long and tapered, suggesting skill. The nail trimmed short so as not to get in the way or scratch or disturb the perfect image of the scene. At times, Bruno wonders how women with such long nails manage, in one respect so un-aesthetic, not good for . . . well, not exactly good for typing.

The girl raises her knees and separates her legs. There's a tiny mole on the inside of her left thigh which looks painted on by some jokester or by a minor French master of the 18th century. An eye-catching detail, like a grain of salt on a guava tart. It would be a crime to cover it with makeup, so the great sorcerer forgives life.

E moves slowly, she knows that right now all Bruno's time—and a healthy check to deposit in the bank—are hers. Besides it's not in her nature to hurry. Run? What for? Hurry? Where's the fire?

E crawls along, delighted. She's slinky, a true whore, she's perfect.

She abruptly raises up to her elbows, looks around, grabs a velvet cushion and places it under her butt.

"Spread your hands," Bruno says. "Let's see what happens."

She poses again and now displays her rosy, slightly moist, bubbly vulva, surrounded by a sumptuous copper down that matches her unshaved armpits. Her little oval—pursed for no apparent reason, there's nothing to be scared of in the studio just like there's no invisible enemy to defy her "no trespassing" sign—her erect lobe, poking out between minute folds. Delicious, firm, visible. You feel the urge to lick it for a long time, to sink your mouth and nose in it.

Bruno thinks nobody ever painted women like that, the way they looked their best. Didn't dare dream of it. They stone artists and destroy their paintings for less. Or hurl it all, artists and paintings, into the bonfire of the vanities. He's always been naive, maybe that explains why he never understands people who think the vanities are bad.

"We photographers have been luckier in our struggle than most artists." He enunciates each word, like an orator, "if you can call it luck. Considering we are the newest artists and we often inhabit the margins of what's holy, we're given some leeway. Pornography and art, there's a fine line between them, each in its place, a label pinned to your back. If nothing's ambiguous, you're safe . . . Why do I think about these things now? Why do I care? I can't stop being who I am—and I don't want to! And I don't want to change anyone else either. There's something immature, something pathetic, and fun in whining like this. Don't think I don't know that."

Getting back to the body on the rug, to the cushion, the fringe on a shawl, her vortex. God, she's beautiful! The whole scene makes him ache to discard his camera. Words almost fail Bruno.

As he studies her, he slowly comes to believe that E would make a great lesbian, celebrated like those at Helen of Troy's fan clubs, or like those budding young girls who graze each other's breasts as they dance, or like Djuna Barnes' almanac of women. Or maybe she's already a lesbian, he hasn't asked her. Surrounded by foam, gauzy see-through clothes and lace, the Sapphic point of view. Bruno would be a happy man if he could somehow slip into those clubs. He'd dress up like a woman if that's what it took. He's a simple man, the kind who thinks the more women, the better. If this pose turns out well . . . Hope springs eternal, like what flies out of the bottom of Pandora's box of evils, spins through the air across the studio, alights on his forehead. Maybe he should suggest to E a couple of sessions with . . .

For the moment, she (E) looks great, wearing her vertical smile . . . an improvement over that other smile. Her ineffable, persistent, almost mystical, mystifying smile. The one that dares to take the leading role smack dab in the center of the flash.

"That's not it. E, that's just not it." Something is wearing him out. "I don't have to develop it to know that's just not it."

The girl gets into a full lotus and looks at him. Sad? Who knows. That sheer makeup suits her, it accentuates her skin color. They're no marks on her skin. Not a blemish, not even a wrinkle or a scar, nothing. Anyone would think she was a virgin, and not the enemy, but more encompassing in a way.

Suddenly he feels the urge to slap her, to wipe that look off her face, the look he doesn't understand and that ruins his work. He counts to ten, breathes. Eleven. It's not enough. He goes back to his thirty five millimeter single lens, his SLR, a mental "Look at the birdie," eighty-five millimeter lens, the lens, another mental birdie, F5.6, F . . .

"You're driving me crazy, y'know that?"

He lights two cigarettes at once and hands her one. He's never seen her smoke, but the little witch takes it docilely.

"Come on, honey, can't you give me some other expression?"

She cocks her head the way a dog does when it sees something strange, as if three very shocking transvestites crossed the desert with their music, high heels and sequins. She watches him through the smoke she barely inhales, she protects herself. Bruno thinks that if he got too close to her, she might bolt, run into the street and get lost in the rain, naked to boot. He thinks he might not be able to catch up with her. Who knows when he'd see her again.

He describes the expression he wants from her, although at this point any grimace would do so long as it doesn't look like the fucking little smile that not even a cigarette can extinguish. It's not easy to describe an expression, even harder when you're dealing with something so subtle, but Bruno gives it a shot. And it makes no sense to show her the other girls' photographs, she shouldn't imitate them, every little witch should let her personality shine through. But isn't that what she's doing? Here our artist gets tangled up again, bites his tongue not to fall back on a beginner's copybook with his mental "birdie."

Outside there's a downpour, thunder here, thunder there, till it forms one magnificent, singular thunder clap overhead. The modest hills of the Vedado neighborhood loom as stormy summits.

"I never claimed I'd stripped a virgin on the rocks, understand? Never!" He didn't mean to shout, but he's shouting. "I've told you a hundred times. I go to Barcelona, to an erotic film festival! The Mostra d'Art is about art. That's right, erotic *art*! Not spiritualistic art, not psychoanalytic art. Erotic art. E-ro-tic art. And that look of yours! Beats the hell out of me what that's all about. You'd make any guy impotent. It's a fucking bucket of cold water! Hold your mouth like this! Look at me!" She hasn't taken her eyes off him for a second. "Like this!"

He makes a face. She cocks her head again. And she lets out a great big belly laugh. Like a little Christmas tree covered with bells, shaken by the wind blowing on the other side of the wall. She laughs so hard she nearly bursts into tears. Her breasts rise and fall in time with her laughter. Then the little smart aleck nearly chokes on the smoke. OK, OK, let her laugh. What can Bruno do? Talking gets him nowhere. He shuts up. He has no choice.

He could drape her red hair over her face. A subtle candle, a landscape you can barely make out behind the flame. That is not ideal but, if there's no alternative . . . Because he's not about to look for another model. No way. Even if he has to wring her neck. She's his, he found her, he picked her out in the street among thousands of flashier women. E: common, brazen, free, he brought her to his studio.

Aside from her thin, but very pretty legs (in the other shoot she's wearing black stockings in several photos, too bad they didn't turn out) what he'd liked most about her, Bruno recalls, was, strangely enough, her smile.

I can't find a way to describe E's smile, to make you see it so you'll understand poor Bruno and not think he's weird. It's not a matter of just pressing the shutter and *presto*. Not everything is photogenic. You could say, perhaps, that it's the smile of someone who has lived through a frightening and wonderful time in her life, a very special adventure, the kind that happens once in a lifetime. The smile of a person who recalls a unique, irreplaceable lover with sarcastic kindness, happy rancor and who knows how many more contradictions.

When Bruno saw her for the first time, how could he have guessed that that smile was clamped on its owner like Monseigneur Louis's iron mask? In the end, does she own the smile or does it own her? It (the smile) didn't attract him as much as what was hidden behind it. How foolish. How could he have guessed it would bother him so much? Because it bothers him a lot: not even the coppery curtain of her hair has had an effect. Another failure. Always the same mistake. Her ghostly smile persists even behind the fire. What's worse: the observer's eye is compelled to intuit, tune out, decipher. He goes no further than her chin.

What if he always photographed her with her back turned? Something interesting might turn out if you don't see her face. That might work. Mystery girl or something like that. Who is she? A famous actress? A neighbor? His assistant? His wife? You decide! To stay calm, Bruno lies to himself. He continues with that train of thought. His mystery girl won't resemble Valpincon's bather, or Velazquez's Venus, the one with the mirror, the best ass of all time. Those women are too famous, too recognizable. Bruno loves mirrors; they fascinate him, and their multiple possibilities stimulate his imagination. But he doesn't try them out with E. Why duplicate what annoys him?

The mystery girl, propped up on her elbows on the rug: her round, slightly flabby buttocks, shockingly flawless, shaped like an upside down heart, an apple or a pear, like the buttocks that chorus girls in the Moulin Rouge bared, the one the dwarf drew. A ring even more pursed than her little oval, warning the invisible enemy: "don't even think about it." Pink like all the pink on her, maybe a bit darker. Her copper-colored down, her vertical smile now backwards, but equally spongy and tempting between two chubby little lips that droop a bit toward the back of the composition, taking advantage of the favorable angle. Her breasts droop, too, like ripe mangos, pointed, the real thing, pre-dating the silicon culture that doesn't do a thing for the great sorcerer.

How slowly she moves, cat-like, her whole body undulating. What Bruno wants now is to kneel behind her, cradle her breasts in his hands, squeeze them, pull them, make them hurt, tickle his palms with her hard nipples—and penetrate her with a hard thrust. Her little oval or ring, either one. Pursed like that, he imagines how they'd squeeze him. How she'd moan, cry out, writhe . . .

He comes back to reality: his studio, his camera and all its attachments, the storm in the street. He comes back, not to high art, like he should, but to E's smile. He can't make out her face, but he can't focus either because, he's surprised to admit, he knows she's smiling. They call that paranoia, don't they? I think so.

I never thought about E as a lover. His, I mean. The model is the observer's lover, what Bruno feels for a few seconds looking at her body is what he'd wanted to transmit to him (or her). He'd never touched her, not out of any moral conviction, but out of his old mania for order, for not mixing business with pleasure. Before, he dreamed of everything he'd do to her when the shoot was over . . . Now he's convinced he'll never go to bed with her.

Something makes her untouchable. It's not her body or what the eye detects in its search for pleasure, but rather something photographs reveal. Maybe the mark of an unknown man that no one can measure up to. What did he do to her, for God's sake, what did he do? He doesn't dare ask. Could she explain it in words? Perhaps, but what good would it do? Something weighs her down, the great sorcerer senses it, the ghost of something indelible, something she's lived through, something that drags her toward dangerous, un-navigable depths and banishes the happy frivolity of his art.

He gives up, exhausted. With as much courtesy as he can muster, he tells her they've finished for the day. He tells her nobody sends anyone packing in the rain, she can stay till it lets up, if she likes. She gets up without a word and walks to the corner farthest from the light where she'd left her clothes very neatly folded on the back of a chair. She doesn't seem upset. Of course not. Why would she be? All the anxiety falls on Bruno's shoulders, he has to deal with it. The shoot's over for today. And tomorrow? What'll he do tomorrow? He hasn't the slightest idea. What's he going to do with you, E? How will he pose you? He's down in the dumps, the enthusiasm he felt at first is gone.

He calls to her and a voice answers him from the corner with the chair and the shadow: "Yes, what is it?"

"E, you realize it isn't going well, don't you?"

"Yes, I realize that. I guess you'll have to find another girl."

"No, E, I don't want another model."

"So, now what? What do you want me to do? You say don't smile, so I don't. I really don't. But you're not satisfied. What do you want from me? You don't let up. You say I keep on smiling. I'm driving you crazy and all that. The problem is you don't like my face . . ."

He interrupts her, "That's not it exactly . . ."

She interrupts him, "Well, something like that. I didn't know my face was that important in this kind of photograph."

"I didn't either. To be honest nothing like this has happened before. But tell me, have you done this before?"

She emerges from the shadows, dressed, with a lit cigarette. Thunder drowns out her "Yes, once. But that was different, very different. *He* liked my face, he liked everything I did." E's eyes shine with a radiance almost as ambiguous as her damned smile.

"Do you still have those pictures? I'd like to take a look at them. If you don't mind."

"I don't mind. I only have one left. The others got lost or were confiscated when everything blew up in our faces. But you're in luck, at least in that way: I always carry it around with me."

She digs around in her leather bag while Bruno asks himself if he is the "he," the unique lover, and he asks her what blew up, in whose face.

"Everything! Everything! People don't understand, you know? There was a trial," she shrugs her shoulders the way the great sorcerer's seen her do so many times over the last few days.

"People said horrible things. Afterwards I lost track," her sigh is full of a very old hatred. "I never heard another word."

She holds out a black and white photo, the size of a postcard, with very ragged edges and curled up corners.

"First time I've shown it to anyone."

Bruno carries it over to the lamp and what he sees catches him off guard. There before his eyes (accustomed, as you might imagine, to all kinds of tricks and lunacy) the light makes the inexorable image of E leap off the page: she's stark naked, stretched out, in a full frontal pose, arms behind her head and one knee flexed so you can see the mole on her thigh and more. Charming, smiling, a little queen, already sure of her power . . . seven or eight years old.

Translation by Pamela Carmell

Women of the Federation

Francisco García González

She's stretched out on her back on the bed and I know she's having
a lousy day. She has the complexion of a fresh apple. Sometimes I
keep this to myself and other times I get a kick out of telling her so,
depending on how things are going. Pretty corny. I'm always thinking it, but I only say it out loud once in a while. I look at the magazine that hides her face. I run my eyes over the sweet fingers of her
sweet hands and the sweet freckles where her shoulders begin and
the sweet breasts drifting toward her armpits. I look at the magazine and I wonder what she can be reading since she only knows
about five words of English. "Goodbye." "Boy." "Girl." Maybe "Nike"
if not "night," because women are so smart—about brand names. I'm
sure she's gazing at the barefoot models or reading the names of the
face creams and vitamins for the skin, or just casting her eyes over
the pictures of overflowing platters of luscious-looking food. She
loves lotions and constantly frets about the sun because her complexion is so fair. She's an active member of the Federation of Cuban
Women, a food service worker, wears a uniform and black stockings,
and, contrary to what you might think or she might hope, she is
always ravenously hungry. I love her complexion and her appetite,
her sweaty sheathed legs. I call her my yummy Pudge, my scrump-
tious pink Piggy, and watch how her nostrils dilate. Because Pudge
or my little Piggy are invocations, triggers that unleash whirlwinds
of desire. Followed by stiffening nipples, pupils rolled back, uncon-
trollable gasping until the spasm of release, feet kicking the air
beneath or on top of me. I give her a whistle, ask how she's doing
just to say something. I see her legs poking out from under the sheet
and her underpants bulging around the double sanitary pads, so I
know it's the third day, when her flow always seems even heavier
than last month's. She doesn't answer. I go into the bathroom. Poor
baby; I know she's having a bad day. I open the window. The book
of word games is on the toilet tank. She's good at word puzzles. She
left the last Find The Word page half done. Topic: soccer. Words to
spot: goal, contract, penalty, score, winger, corner, line . . . I reach
into the hamper and touch her soiled clothes. I pull out her work
stockings and some white panties, yellowed by pee stains. I suck in
my breath until my lungs are filled. Man, this is my girl's smell. I
look around for the toothpaste and my toothbrush among the empty
face cream jars and shampoo bottles, then I go back to smelling
those yellow pee stains on her panties and I think how intimate and

tender my girl's world is. Sometimes I'm part of her world, but other times I feel like an intruder. I give my dick a shake and the last drops spill onto the floor and onto the edges of the toilet. Pudge threatens that someday she'll stick a hose onto me every time I take a leak. Men's pee stinks worse than women's, she claims, and she says I manage to drip all over the place so it reeks like a bus station latrine. That's what she says and I get a kick out of thinking how wise women are and how they can do everything better. I finish brushing my teeth and count the napkins in the open packet: Pudge should have enough for this month. She's still got one more unopened packet. So she'll get by until next time. It doesn't help to tell her to think positively. She's cheerful, even joyful and optimistic, until two days before the cataclysm strikes. And then, all of a sudden, she wakes up one day and her breath smells different and she's got that look on her face that neither one of us likes. And sure enough, the next day the bleeding starts. Spotting at first and then a heavy flow, with clots in it. I've seen them on the tiles in the shower and in the toilet bowl when the water's off. The image of a clot on a tile floor is the very embodiment of abandonment and desolation. But a clot floating in water is something else, it remains diaphanous and intact even while those little protuberances like the pseudopodia of a handsome amoeba are swaying around. With time it begins to dissolve and tints the water until it becomes an intense purple as the clot disappears. It's beautiful. She finds it disgusting. I like it, but I don't tell her so, any more than I tell her I smell her panties, pee stained and unwashed. I leave the towel on the rod and count the napkins in the packet again, and the used ones in the waste basket. The total, figuring in the two she has on, confirms my guess: she'll have enough for this month. So that's good. I stand on the scale. From the bathroom I can see the magazine and her fingers. She's lying on her back on the bed and I know she's having a lousy day. I give her a whistle, but she doesn't answer. She goes on gazing at the barefoot models and the delicious platters of food, even though I can't imagine that she's feeling very hungry right now. On days like this I exempt her from everything. Pudge, I'll make my own breakfast, and I'll leave a nice lunch all ready for you, and you can just stay there in bed until I get back, my lady love, my madonna, my nymph, and that way you can listen to the soap operas and watch the noon preview programs and finish your word game and listen to all the tapes you want. Anything, Pudge, just don't look out the window to see if the smokestack off in the distance is belching smoke up into the sky or if it remains silent and lifeless, shut down yet again. Because, Pudge, today is a gray day which is doubly bad for you, so tell the world to go to hell and just stay here resting until your *papi* comes back. I never knew what that distant chimney was until she

moved in with me. It was during our first menstrual period together. On the third day I found her on her knees, gazing out the window.
She gestured for me to come over and asked me if I knew what that
chimney was, the one we could see in the distance between the gray
stone buildings. And here I'd been thinking that she was engrossed
in the trees in the park, or was watching the kids running around
benches in the little plaza. "That's the smokestack of the sanitary
pad factory." I looked and saw how lifeless it was, without a single
plume of smoke against the sky. She didn't have to explain anything
to me. I rinse out the glass and go back into the bathroom. A new
pad count, more drops on the floor and on the edge of the toilet bowl,
again the fragrance of Pudge's pee. She gives me a hug and says not
to be late, I tell her I'll call her at noon. I feel her fetid, familiar
breath on me and I think if a guy can feel desire for someone who
smells this bad, he should be called a hero. I avoid the second kiss
with a loving bite on her right ear and I tell her that I can't wait to
get past the next few days so I can nibble on her little ear again and
see her panting with her eyes rolled up. She believes me and hugs
me and I believe me too and I hug her back and I don't avoid the
third kiss because I am a hero and tomorrow or this afternoon I'll
desire Pudge even though she doesn't like it this way in the midst
of so much blood. And in the midst of the kiss and hug it occurs to
me that if, as we've been taught, heroism is based on the amount of
blood spilled for a worthwhile cause, among other things, then women
are the true heroines. The fact that they menstruate just because
they are what they are, well, we men should not only tip our hats,
but take them off altogether. They are the true heroines, women are,
and I shouldn't say I'm a hero just for breathing in her infernal
stinking breath. What does it matter that women, at least some
women, turn on the tears easily. At first, every time we'd find ourselves at the climactic moment of the primordial act, Pudge would
burst into tears. Her sobs drained my enthusiasm and I'd lose my
momentum. I never figured out whether she meant it or not. If it was
a farce, I was sorry I was taking it seriously, and if it wasn't, it was
just too pathetic. The only interesting part was the taste of her
tears: the salty sweetness of a landlocked sea. But all that spilled
blood, and having to put up with it! Pudge, I forgive you the ocean
and for drowning me in your eyes. The topic gets me hot again, and
Pudge complains that I could break her thorax. I blow her a kiss
from the doorway and she tells me to watch out for cars. I blow her
another kiss. She's the one having a lousy day, not her bicyclist.

Pudge isn't pudgy at all, and she has apple skin and she's a heroine because of all that spilled blood.

But the street is something else, man. Another part of the same
thing. The air is just right today because the cold wind has blown

away the last of the fog. This is something only a cyclist would notice. He's on a bike. She's on a bike. They're on bikes. So are we, so are you. The asshole pal—who passed down his bike to me when he decided to leave—is still up there in the States, far away, and since he's a sentimental guy he writes to me once in a while. In his last letter, he told me about how he'd had a dream where I was riding my, *his*, bike thinking about fucking every woman who crossed my path. Just then, like those things that happen in dreams, the person who crossed my path was the Pope, who was here on a visit. A truck goes by almost sideswiping my bike and leaves me wrapped in a dense cloud of black fumes. The guys riding in the back yell at me—either they want to encourage me or else they're just making sure I notice that they're moving a lot faster than the guy they're leaving in the dust. It's a show of strength. "*Tarrú*," I manage to make out, "Asshole!" In the dream of the pal who left me the bike, nothing else happened. I think about what it would be like to meet the Pope somewhere along this highway. His Holiness the Pontiff comes along in his special popemobile, going the opposite direction, and some-thing—he never told me what—makes him notice me. His motorcade comes to a halt. The sun gleams on the keys of the Saint Peter's emblem on his limousine. His aides lead me over to the Vicar and I try to act as natural as possible. He still hasn't opened his mouth and I ask him how's he doing and what's he doing on this highway. He tells me he's going to the hospital, because today is the day of his encounter with the world of pain. Then he asks about my bicycle and I tell him that it was left to me by an asshole pal who feels bad every time he remembers that he had no choice but to go off and leave me this pile of shit, this junk heap. Junkip? His Holiness asks what "junkip" means. I explain to him and his mouth twitches in what looks like a laugh. Then he asks where the owner of the "junkip" (like that, all one word) is and says something about the grievous separation of the family. He too had had to pedal hard in Krakow. I laugh thinking about the Pope having to ride a bicycle back then, and in Krakow because it's the only city in Poland, besides Warsaw, that I've heard people talking about. If the Pope and I met, there'd be lots of photos. Before he went on, he asked me first if I've been baptized by the Holy Mother Church and I tell him yes, I was, and he says that will do. And then, if I fear God. Yes, sir, sometimes I'm scared of God. That, too, is sufficient. Since the motorcade is going in the opposite direction, to its encounter with the world of pain, no one offers to give me a tow. The Pontiff makes one more joke about my "junkip" (like that, all one word). I should skip over the fact that one of the aides gave me a T-shirt with Saint Peter's keys on it and a cloth patch with the image of Mary on it. Once again, the same fumes on the road and the same or other shirtless black guys are yelling at me. This time I do understand. There, from the truck, a proletarian-truck, the black guys yell that I'm an asshole and that I should get out of the way and they're also going in the opposite direction from the Pontiff. Although they (the black guys) and I are going along another road (which is the same one, not the only one) toward the world of pain. And what if I'd told the Pontiff that my girl is home in bed and if I'd told him about the sanitary pads and about the worst days when my heroine just stays in bed? For sure he'd scratch one ear and would recommend me to his pupil, Mother Teresa, who might well be here and not so far away, unreachable Mother of Calcutta. Today the north wind has blown off the fog and the wind shoves me along, and I catch up with other cyclists. An old man. Another old man. A guy with a bored expression, even though the north wind pushes him the same as yesterday and tomorrow. By now Pudge has probably tired of her magazine and gone back to the Find A Word game. Penalty. Contract. Run. Goal. Pudge is really good at finding the words. The cyclists are left behind and the bright, soft sun, cooled by the north wind, gleams not on the emblem of Saint Peter's keys, but on the roadside stand where they sell cane juice, *guarapo,* to people coming and going along the highway. I might invite the Pontiff to have a *guarapo* with me. I'll bet no Pope has ever had a *guarapo.* The Pontiff's in luck: they have ice. I order two *guarapos.* The kiosk owners refuse to charge the visitor. His Holiness admires the machinery that crushes the cane and spits the stalks out in bits. The owners recommend we add lemon. We do so. Tasty. Delicious. The aides try the drink, too. The owners tell the Pontiff that they work in a cooperative named "Cuba-Laos Friendship." Cuba-Laos Friendship? Wow, he says to me, that must be very important. It is. I ask the owners if they know where Laos is, and they answer that they do not, that when they got there, that was the name of the place. I understand, says the Pontiff. This machine is a "junkip" (like that, all one word). We all laugh. I almost laugh and I finish drinking the *guarapo.* No ice today, the guy in the cap tells a taxi driver. Did any Pope ever really drink *guarapo?* What will the friend who left me the bike think if I tell him how I've improved upon his dream? The taxi driver doesn't much like warm *guarapo,* either, so he orders just one. While he drinks, he notices that the business belongs to the "Cuba-Laos Friendship" cooperative. He asks about it. No clue, pal, when we got here the place was already named that. The taxi driver and I pay. Tomorrow there will be ice, then we'll each have two and eventually someone will tell the owners where Laos is. Tomorrow or never.

The other item in my friend's dream isn't quite true. While I pedal along, I'm not thinking that I want to go to bed with every woman who comes into view. I'd have gone to bed with Pudge if today were a good day for her. And there are no women hitchhiking, standing in the shade of the trees along the side of the road. No. It's Lisanka I'm thinking of. I should admit it, the dream is partly about her. I've given Lisanka the best thrusts of all in my mind and on this bicycle. Once I told her about it and she told me I had a sick mind and that's what she liked about me. Lisanka is different from Pudge. At least that gives our relationship some meaning. Otherwise, why bother? I met Lisanka not long ago on a bus. I met Pudge at some friends' house. When I saw Lisanka hanging onto the bar trying to read a book, I stood right behind her, leaving just enough space so it could be accidental or on purpose on my part. It was a book of poetry. "If everyone riding a bus read a book, we'd be closer to the sun." She laughed. You couldn't begin on a higher note. The day I met Pudge, I had to use the bathroom. That underwear couldn't belong to anyone else. The olfactory memory, the girl they had introduced me to had to be menstruating. That may not have been her day, and that's why she hardly paid any attention to me, there are meetings and then there are meetings. Lisanka tells me not to exaggerate, the fact is we were pretty close to the sun in that bus, otherwise why would we have been sweating so much. And since sometimes I manage some mental agility, I scolded her and said she shouldn't confuse hell with the sun. In hell, it could be cold, too. Cold and hot. I asked her to read me a poem. Just then we were pressed tight against each other. Lisanka closed the book. *If some day the waters / drown my memory / from the first scolding / to the final holocaust* . . . the poem was hers. Lisanka belonged to the "Rabindranath Tagore" literary workshop. Lisanka was a writer. Pudge was studying gastronomic science when we met. The day after we met, she had a practical exam and had to present a main dish. She was complaining that she wanted to make stuffed peppers and she couldn't find the two peppers anywhere. Everyone in the room was complaining. Pudge never suspected that her smell and her skin interested me. I offered to look for the peppers. They tried gently to dissuade me: it was a pretty risky business. Pudge was having a really bad day. Lisanka said that Rabindranath Tagore was a Turkish poet with a very long beard. I could get into that. *Like the pocked sea / the waves boiled / in such gray display / close by other rocks.* You just can't let a poet with such an elevated idea of Turkish poets get away. I pressed her on the nationality of the poet. Right. Turkey, over there by India. If I hadn't seen her eyes I'd have thought Lisanka might be leading me on. But Lisanka is incapable of lying, I picked up on that right away. Rabindranath Tagore was Turkish, from over there by India. Women do things that just kill you. I didn't wait for my bus stop. Want to go sit in the park? Lisanka's skin was white with delicate black fuzz on it. It was a risky enterprise, something that added to her attractions.

I spent the afternoon walking the city, and Pudge ended up with not two but five handsome peppers. Under the trees, Lisanka read the poem again . . . *And perhaps you will arrive invading / before and after, you / alone at the helm, your back to time.* Things wouldn't—a question of chance—have progressed past the enchantment of listening to each other, if Lisanka hadn't revealed the mystery of her name. Lisanka was the name of the mare that belonged to a character in a Soviet novel, a book we'd all read in the crowded military barracks in the '60s. *Whipping his gallop / quick to retreat / like the pocked sea.* A shame not to be the Ivan or Boris who could go for a gallop on this Lisanka. The woman laughed and I thought how long her face was, and what big, strong teeth she had, and what a black and gleaming mane. And the image of desire was a woman-mare who wrote poems and trotted in the solitude of my bicycle journeys. But I knew that no matter how much the poet aroused me with her neighing, it was my displaced apple I really wanted to bed, although sometimes with desire stimulated elsewhere. A week after the exam, Pudge came to my house and repeated every detail of the exam in my kitchen, barefoot and aproned. Pudge laughed her way around the house, inspecting and tidying up. I followed her around because I was so taken with her legs and her barefootedness, until she stopped in front of the window and pointed at the dreary smokeless chimney. She didn't explain then what it was about. I'd rather gallop and savor an apple, says a banal—that is, astute—pop tune.

I swerve around an ambulance and turn my attention back to my pal's dream. I had never thought so much about a Pontiff before. We ordered two *guarapo*s and stood back from the counter. Behind the *guarapo* stand, the slaughterhouse butchers of the "Cuba-Laos Friendship" cooperative have done their usual stuff. Right by our feet runs a stream of water red with the blood of just-butchered hogs. I'm afraid my guest will ruin his white cassock on his day to visit the world of pain. We stand there looking at the blood, and I'm sure his thoughts flow toward the earth where the blood will turn to dust tomorrow or the next day. And maybe because I see him so deep in thought, I ask him if by any chance he remembers a Soviet novel where a character had a mare named Lisanka. He sighs, stands there gazing at his glass, and then confesses that he has never been able to get through a Soviet novel. I trade confessions with him: I haven't either. What do you think we've missed, Your Holiness? What do you think we've been spared, son? Eating apples? A good gallop?

The street is one thing and work is quite another, man. I don't know who the hell this "man" is. It's not Pope John Paul or my bicycle buddy. The secretary has left me a note. She's had to go to the hospital with an asthma attack and won't be back until afternoon. Clients won't come either, which makes me pretty happy. You can expect all the extremes of behavior, good and bad, from these guys, never the normal thing. I shuffle through my papers and a picture of my pal with the bicycle falls out onto the floor. He rode that bike to work for two years. He had a job in a cemetery. When he walked into his office to deal with death, he'd say hello to the woman in charge of death certificates. At noon, she'd come in and they'd screw on his desk. She complained about this a little. Afterward, they'd pee in a potted plant. The plant seemed to thrive on this. It's complicated, but we've kept in touch. He's never met Pudge. I'd like to tell him about Lisanka and her poems, about how, contrary to all expectation, we've never gone beyond some affectionate making out, even though my ideal fantasy is the woman-mare strumming a harp and neighing in my ears. Ah, Lisanka's mouth. On the back of the picture, my pal wrote that someday we'll have to compare notes. He's put on so much weight that he looks like a different person. He and Pudge could cook up some good dishes in the kitchen. What would it be like to have a three-way conversation between him, the Pope, and the heir of the bicycle? We'd talk and we'd drink *guarapo*, watching the blood—the hogs' blood—run along the side of the road until it soaked into the earth and the dust. For sure we'd tell two or three good jokes that we'd have to explain to the priest. I put the picture and the papers away. I take a look at the newspaper. Italian Robbers Drugged Their Victims. Police detained four Albanians who had been breaking into victims' houses, and knocking them out with drugs so they could get away with all kinds of bad stuff. Rape, robbery. New members appointed to the Socialist International. Alleged fraud in Special Oympics disputed in Mexico City. "Troyano" disguised as Y2K error. Called FIX2001, the virus infiltrates computers, disguised as innocent electronic message. Before I folded the paper back up, a letter to the editor caught my attention. A lady's companion has gone from one province to another on account of a death in her family. The wake has made her realize that coffin manufacturing is a disaster in her town, while at the same time she praises the good taste and efficiency of the operations of the funeral home that tended to her relative. The list of manufacturers' shortcomings in her native Guantánamo fall like hammer blows on stone. Green wood. Skimping on nails. Poor quality lining cloth. Delays in delivery to the family. A shoddy product. Her complaint is going to the sanitary authorities of her town. She ends by congratulating her colleagues in Bijarú. Bijarú: now there's a place where they know how to treat you right on your final journey. Bitter words from a *compañera* now sitting in her armchair, sipping coffee after coffee. The moment comes for us all, and one coffin is not the same as any other. We want to do it right when we die. A letter like this merits serious action. This heroine, apart from the blood she has spilled during her life, is the defender of a cause that is surely transcendent. I cut the letter out carefully. I'll send it to my bicycle buddy, so he can see. Better to send him the entire paper. I put water on to boil. Just as I put the kettle on, the electricity goes off. I look over the clients' requests one more time. It would be better if they didn't come, at least not today. At first sight, the operation doesn't seem complicated. I go through the document and by the end I can hardly believe how tortuous and eccentric a procedure it is. New winds of consumer awareness are blowing. Someday everyone everywhere will have coffins like the ones in Bijarú. At noon I call my heroine. Nothing new, the word search for soccer terms is giving her a headache. I cheer her up by suggesting that she look for a topic she likes better. Before hanging up she reminds me to bring her the magazine with the article about Lady Di's death, she wants to read it again and loan it to some friends. The day they issued Cuban stamps with Diana on them, Pudge wanted me to get her some. Neither one of us has ever collected a stamp. The Diana stamps are under the glass top of the dresser with some postcards of the movie *Titanic*. I promise her I won't be late and I'll bring her the magazine. A little while later the phone rings. Neighing on the other end, that seductive voice reels me in. Lisanka is alone and wants me to have lunch with her. I feel like I'm throwing myself off the top of a roller coaster. I feel bad about Pudge, but the poet mare is the vivid, single image of desire right this instant. Despite her pleas, I detect a sad tone in her voice. I'm a pushover. There's a silence after we hang up. Behind the indecipherable noise lurks surprise and the mystery of poems I'll never understand. I feel bad again. Without victims or perpetrators, how could heroines exist?

The street is one thing, and work something else, and this chasing after another woman, can't even talk about that one, man. I hadn't seen or talked to Lisanka for three days. Down the roller coaster I slide, and my hard-on is the bicycle's horse. Nothing matters, not her sad tone of voice, not the war in my diaphragm, not Pudge or the Pope or the dust soaking up the blood spilled by the slaughterhouse butchers and by my heroines. This chasing after another woman, man. This hiding my desperation when I get to her door. The exquisite detail of Lisanka's white fingers on the brass doorknob. "Hi there." The silky mane brushes against my cheeks and the scent, that distinctive scent of this Lisanka, who stands there with her hand on the knob, tells me her body fluids are awash in an elemental mix of woman and beast. Down the roller coaster, man. Excuses, but there's no action brewing here, nothing to excuse. And before Lisanka even says a word, I know, feel sure of it, that today's not her day. Lunch was just a pretext, even though the french fries, canned meat, rice and beans, and the two beers are right there. I dish some up for her and help myself. Great potatoes and meat, and Lisanka watches me

chew as though seeing me eat were a banquet for her. Today is not
her day. Yeah, I know, I tell her. She smells different. The Soviet
hero's mare runs her fingertip through the sweat on the glass. The
mare isn't hungry. Her parents get home tomorrow. She asks me if I
think she's fat and if I want her lunch, she doesn't feel well. It's all
a terribly domestic, and even heroic, scene. I feel the tension in my
diaphragm subsiding. Will Lisanka's clots, on the bathroom tiles, be
the very image of desolation or will they waft like beautiful amoebas
in the water in the toilet bowl? I tell her it's fine with me and I'm
glad she felt she could call me when she feels this way. I get her to
stand up and I pull her onto my lap. Lisanka relaxes against my body,
I stroke her mane and she lifts my hand to her lips. She kisses my
fingers. She bites them with her square, equine teeth. If she has
called me today, it's because she takes me seriously, she assures me
and that, for now, seems OK to me. She has several things to tell
me. Things she can't tell anyone else. On days like this, she thinks
nothing she does matters. The last poem she read at the "Rabindranath Tagore" workshop, named for the Turkish poet, was a great
success. But she doesn't believe it. *This December day, / the forest is
so heavy / it hides mockingly / amidst sips of solitude.* How can she
have any doubt about such moving images. The weight of a forest
hiding mockingly. Lisanka shouldn't even question the beauty of
something like that, I assure her, hugging her. And it's not that I'm
being an asshole, leading her on, but right this moment, a heavy
forest hiding mockingly amidst sips of solitudes are words that
embody a beauty that is total, possible . . . *often piling up debris /
beside old ants / hanging from my eyes.* I think Lisanka has talent,
and I hug her close again with my arms that have been the victims
of simultaneous natural cycles. Lisanka's weight on my knees begins
to bother me. *Sustained by the gaze / of sterile rains.* We kiss, a key
move, man, when you're trying to keep from inhaling bad breath.
Perhaps wisely / I could bear no more. Man, I like this poem, what
does it matter whether R. T. is Turkish or Malay or Australian. I
move out from under Lisanka's weight. In vain, I look in the bathroom for trophy by-products, the package with whatever napkins are
left, clots, old pee-stained underpants. Then we sit on the bed. Will
the day ever come when we won't doubt what we do? Doubt has no
sex, Lisanka. I've written a story, too. A story, Lisanka? It's called
"Blame the river." Hardly letting me ask about it, the mare cleared
the next hurdle without a hitch. Marisol meets Miguel at a meeting,
Marisol goes to live at the guy's house. One day, without any explanation, Miguel commits suicide. Marisol, who is pregnant, is rejected
by Miguel's parents. She goes to see the dead man's aunt and uncle.
Miguel was HIV positive. Shock. Then I . . . ? Positive. Marisol-
Ophelia-Alfonsina Storni (the river connection), instead of heading

home to her parents, leaps into the river believing that she sees Miguel's face in a small, luminous window in the middle of the rapids. Miguel is calling her: "Come on, darling, come on." Marisol-Alfonsina-Ophelia doesn't know how to swim. The end. She hasn't read the story yet in the R. T. Workshop. I scratch my head. Lisanka is waiting for my reaction. I don't know, right on the spot. I'd have to reread it. You should let me have it, and tomorrow I'll tell you. Lisanka moves her ears and her mane. From this angle she looks more attractive. We fall into each other's arms again. I liked your story, but I don't know. The heroine opens her legs and makes space for me down there. We can't do this, I don't feel well. You don't have to tell me, Lisanka, today's a bad day for everyone. About that guy with AIDS, that's strong stuff, man. Strong stuff. The heroine pushes me away slowly: now my weight bothers her. I go back to variations on my buddy's dream. The Pontiff swirls his *guarapo* around. The hogs' blood runs right by our feet. All rivers flow into the sea. Even the one Marisol leapt into, without first checking with the Center for Hygiene and Epidemiology just in case. I tell the priest I'd like to confide in him. I'm attracted to two women, sir. My guest finished his drink and shrugged his shoulders. There's sin along all of life's roads, son. He tells me this, he, a priest, a man, an old man. Then he says goodbye to me through the window of the popemobile. At my side, my pal drinks his *guarapo*. It's been years since I've had such good *guarapo*. We both gaze at the mix of blood and water running into the ditch. Cuba and Laos can do a lot together. No one laughs. I tell my pal I'd like to confide in him. I'm attracted to two women, bro. My pal finishes his drink and shrugs his shoulders. Don't leave the main road for a detour, my friend. He's saying this as a man who's monogamous and who's seen the sun set over the mouth of the Hudson River. I get off of Lisanka. We'll have our trot another day. That's strong stuff about AIDS, man. Nothing more demoralizing, man, than AIDS and pornography. The one castrates you, and the other is too perfect, and excludes you. Now Lisanka can breathe better and asks me what kind of music I'd like. The mare walks past me and her strong odor hits me in the stomach. Anyone who is capable of desiring someone who stinks like this is either a hero or out of his mind. This is the second time I've thought this. And while Lisanka fusses over the music, I inflate a condom and paint little eyes on it, and a smile, and an "I Love Lisanka" and below that, the head of a mare with very long eyelashes. When Lisanka comes back, I toss the zeppelin into the air. The poet neighs with pleasure and I'm glad she's pleased. We play a little volleyball. A condom, man. A condom for Lisanka. I hear the sound of Silvio Rodrígues on the record player. I tell Lisanka I didn't think anyone paid attention to Silvio Rodrígues any longer. I think he's great. I bet you do—I can't stand him, I think he's really trite. How could I have guessed that such a casual remark would upset her so. I got tangled in a stupid explanation and I finally said she was right. Silvio Rodrígues is a great guy. If my friend the midget heard you, he'd throw a brick at your head. The midget, Lisanka? But no one else counts here but us, and certainly not a midget, right, my mare? *How could it be / how could it be / a steed without a rider* . . . A great guy, Lisanka, just like that midget who heaves bricks. Anything you want. Silvio Rodrígues is the best Turkish crooner I know, no matter what the midget says. Anything you want, go on and bleed today, and tomorrow then, we'll get on with it with spurs and riding boots and the bridle that's . . .

The breeze wafts the condom from one side of the room to the other. Lisanka goes back to bed, her ovaries are still aching. She's glad I'm keeping her company. With her legs half open and lying on her back, obviously every month she wishes the earth would swallow her up. Again she apologizes for taking advantage of my patience and my time. I tell her that if it were up to me, I'd spend all afternoon with her, but I'd better get back to work. Just a minute, and the mare heaves up on her haunches and goes over to the cupboard. Help me, would you, before you go. Lisanka spreads a sheet on the bed. If she cuts it into strips, she'll have enough for the rest of this period and next month, too. OK. We set to work. If the Pontiff and the pal with the bicycle saw us, they'd for sure insist on the road of life, sin and the detour. Two heroines are too much. So far Pudge-Apple hasn't had to resort to this extreme. We finally count up sixty strips. At this rate, I'll sleep on the bare mattress, she tells me, and it sounds frivolous and absurd to me. As absurd as asking the Pope in the middle of the highway how things are going. Once again in each other's arms. Pats on the haunch. The heroine will end up with no sheets. If I offered her Pudge's contacts for buying contraband napkins or cotton, it would be a double betrayal. One is enough. And before I leave, I go over to the window and I ask her if she sees that tall tower there in the distance. Well, that's a sanitary products factory, they make napkins. *White on the outside close up / not from far away* . . .

I leave and Lisanka remains standing in the window. I look from the street and to my surprise the smokestack begins to emit swirls of smoke. Then on my bicycle without a Pontiff and without a pal, without *guarapo* or seeing the blood run along the earth, I think about what I'm like, an it seems to me that I, too, am the very image of abandonment. A clot on the tiles, an inflated condom, pulled here, pushed there, pushed and pulled. It's all one thing, man, and this is something else.

Translation by Mary G. Berg

Mirages of Daily Life

Alexis Sebastián García Somodevilla

The Buildings

The trucks pulled up by a vacant lot that was yellowed and covered with caked sludge. Just looking at it gave you a backache. When he looked more closely at the nearby houses, Daniel remembered that a long time ago, in that same place, he'd worked on building some houses. But he could be wrong about that, since he hadn't been a bricklayer for long then, and when he thought about it all these places looked pretty much alike anyway.

Just to make sure, he asked one of the guys right after they got out of the truck:

"Hey, weren't we here before?"

The guy nodded as he looked around the lot indifferently.

"And the houses we built—where'd they go?"

"They've disappeared," the guy said.

"What do you mean disappeared? Who can steal a building?"

"No one has to steal them. They just disappear." the guy said, sounding almost amused.

"So we're just working for the hell of it?"

"Of course not. We get paid. Don't you get paid every two weeks?"

"Yes, but that . . ."

"So what if the buildings disappear? Even if we don't come back to this site, we'll keep putting them up in different places. Unless you get a different job."

"Is there any job where things don't just disappear?"

Suddenly Daniel's fellow worker turned very serious.

"Look, kid," he said to him, "don't complicate my life. Think whatever you want to think. Either way, I'm going on vacation tomorrow."

The Punching Bag

The police car screeched to a stop and backed up. When the car was right across from Daniel, the cops got out.

Daniel stood up, worried. It's true that at that hour of night you weren't supposed to be stretched out on a bench.

"What are you smoking?" asked one cop, grabbing at a twig sticking out of Daniel's mouth.

"Smoking? I'm not smoking anything."

"What have you got in here?" asked the cop as he pulled open the backpack.

"It's sawdust for a punching bag."

The cop dumped all the sawdust out of the pack.

"What're you practicing for?"

"Nothing. I do it to unwind. I hit it with whatever comes to hand. A stick, a rock, a pole, anything."

"To unwind from what?" asked the cop.

Daniel made a vague gesture with his hands. They were staring hard at him.

"To unwind from whatever. You know how it is. Tension, too much work, all that . . . you know."

The cops turned their backs on him and got back into the car.

Daniel watched with relief as they sped off.

The Chimney Sweep

Any chimney sweep's destiny is the destiny of all chimney sweeps. No one can change that. To change it would be to steal the secret of such a noble job, to snatch the broom and the ladder from the chimney sweep and throw him into the water. And what good is a chimney sweep in the water? Usually they drown. The truth is, they don't know how to swim.

Because of this, when as small children they go up to the rooftop and start talking about chimneys, the best thing their parents can do is encourage their inclination and send them to a chimney sweeping school. They will ask to go. They will keep asking until you send them.

The chimney sweep in our story was like the others, but a bit more talented at climbing trees, especially fruit trees. He finished the chimney sweep schools for beginners and continued in the advanced schools, which dealt with huge chimneys. He was very diligent. He practiced every day, and even a cat would have a hard time beating his agility on a rooftop. Finally he completed his studies. He finished them while he was still young and returned home triumphantly, with all sorts of awards and a diploma bordered in gold.

The welcome he received was extraordinary. The boy came home a man, a man with useful skills. His diploma said "Chimney Sweep, Specialist in Heights" and they hung it on the wall. He hardly got a chance to sleep because so many people came around wanting to see it. They'd come bursting in the door rudely and stand staring at the certificate. Everyone in the family knew that there weren't many expert chimney sweeps and even though he had not yet started his work, he promised to be one of the very good ones.

But disappointment wasn't long in coming.

The first day the chimney sweep went out to work, he couldn't find a single chimney anywhere. Not one. He confirmed this by standing on the roof of the tallest building in the city and looking in all directions. Furious, he went back home and he asked his parents what it meant. They told him it couldn't be, that if there were schools for chimney sweeps, it was because there were chimneys to clean and if he couldn't see them it must be due to poor vision. They recommended that he go see an eye doctor. But since the chimney sweep knew his eyesight was fine, he didn't waste his time – he went out to the street and asked all the people who walked by. The results were similar. They pointed out invisible chimneys.

His inquiries continued until the inevitable happened: he was taken to a psychiatrist and sent to live in an asylum.

When he got over the shock, he found himself surrounded by truly insane people, dreadful cries and strange conversations. Every morning they forced him to walk around a muddy lawn with some empty benches in the center. It was the usual punishment for annoying the guards.

But our friend soon discovered that he wasn't alone. Several men from his class and others who had graduated earlier were there. He learned that many chimney sweeps lived in the asylum and that more continued to arrive from all over. His case was not unique. They had all manifested the same symptoms before being sent there.

You probably think that life in the asylum was terribly boring for the chimney sweeps, but nothing could be farther from the truth. I mean that there they were actually able to do something. In the kitchen there was a red brick chimney, not too tall, that had been constructed by the first chimney sweeps who'd been sent there. It was behind a wooden shack, and it gave off the whitest, cleanest smoke imaginable.

A great crowd of chimney sweeps were lined up outside the shack, waiting for their turn to clean the chimney.

Translation by Mary G. Berg

The Green Violinist, After Chagall

Anna Lidia Vega Serova

Now that I've found you,
Known you, lived you,
Why are you leaving,
Love?

Mornings, she could be seen out on her balcony with her birds and her plants. She wore thick Coke bottle glasses and a stupid hairdo. Every day she'd greet us with the same smile that seemed somehow snooty, as she went by with her violin in its case on her way to her job as a receptionist at the cultural center.

We're pretty sure she doesn't play the violin. At least, no one's ever heard her. "What a dried-up old maid," we'd say to each other.

When she moved into the building, people began to check her out, but we didn't find out a thing. No one ever took a step through her door.

That's why the whole neighborhood was in an uproar when we saw her with that Chilean or Argentinean (we couldn't figure out which). They went in and closed the door. Then we got into the building just across the street, someone brought some binoculars, and we saw them sitting across from each other talking. He was talking; she was looking at him through those Coke bottle lenses, mechanically smoothing her unsmoothable hair. After about two hours we got really excited: she brought a bottle and two glasses out of the kitchen and began to talk. They changed places; now they were sitting next to each other. We almost got into a fight over the binoculars. The most daring of us were betting that he'd be on top of her in a half hour. The skeptics were a minority. The binoculars went from hand to hand. We were disappointed: when they stood up and we assumed they were about to get to it, but what they did was head for the front door.

We went on talking, trying to figure it out, and when we saw the two of them come out, we decided to send a group to follow them. We were annoyed that they were moving so slowly, but nobody wanted to miss the show.

They say they went to the beach. He was carrying his wine in his hand, and she had her useless violin. Some say that they heard them saying really stupid things about human nature and that stuff, but I think that's a lie: no one can overhear what's said two hundred meters away on a noisy evening. They sat on the seawall, and he put his arm around her shoulders. When it got dark, she took out her violin, but he was the one who played it. They say it was one of those Mozart things you hear on Radio Encyclopedia. Then they went back. Most of us went home at this point, but a few of us stayed to see what would happen. They talked. All they did was talk. Around five, we went off to sleep, but by eight some of us showed up to cover them again. What we saw startled us and amazed us. She was on the balcony without her glasses, with her hair loose and a pink bathrobe that revealed her you know whats. She was smiling. She leaned over and greeted us, asking:

"Is there going to be okra in the market?" Lord knows what okra has to do with all this! He was helping her with the birds and the plants.

A little later she went off with her shopping bags in the direction of the market, smiling and humming to herself. She walked by us and took our breath away. What a woman! There was no way to prove it, but we decided that they must have done it. A woman doesn't change completely overnight just by talking. A moment later a guy came along. We didn't like the look of him. He asked where she lived and we had to tell him. We found out what he does: he's a musician. He plays in a group that practices at a cultural center and he's traveled a lot. The foreigner opened the door to him when he knocked and they started hugging each other like old friends. Pretty soon the foreigner grabbed his backpack, left a paper on the night table and went off with the musician. Some say it was his photo he left, others say it was dollars or maybe his card. What we know for sure is that they walked right past us saying things like "remember so-and-so?" and "how's old Joe doing?"

She came back from the market smiling and humming with two shopping bags packed full. We tried to help her but she said "they're not heavy," and it was as though she didn't really think they were weighing her down. She was floating.

She knocked on the door, waited a moment, and still smiling, opened it with her key. She lugged the bags in, looking in all the corners. When she saw the paper, tomatoes, oranges and everything else went spilling all over the floor.

We felt really bad about this and we wanted to help her, but she wouldn't open the door. Some of us peeked in to see what was going on. There she was, sitting on the floor with the fruit all around her. They said she wasn't crying.

That afternoon the woman in the other stairwell got into a big fight with her mother-in-law and we gave up on the old maid, who is still living there now with her birds, her plants, her Coke bottle glasses and that stupid hairdo that keeps people at least ten feet away from her all around.

She carries the violin upstairs and down again, but we know perfectly well that she doesn't play the violin.

Translation by Mary G. Berg

Paper Love

Anna Lidia Vega Serova

For María Gala, my inspiration

The smell of dampness, of rancidness, of cold sweat, of ancient corruption. The mother puts her little girl to sleep in the room's only bed, the same bed where she'll receive whichever lover comes tonight. She turns out the light, she gropes her way in the dark, she undresses, opens the door a crack. Everything is odors, whispering voices, the muffled creaking of the mattress, rocking and throbbing.

The child falls asleep right away. Her mother won't allow her to wake up, but still, she does: every night she wakes up for an instant when the bed suddenly stops rocking, always abruptly. She hears the heavy breathing beside her, she listens to her heartbeats growing louder and expanding through her body, and the bitter stench and the panic. But she doesn't move; she hardly breathes; she doesn't dare confront her mother's anger.

During the day she looks around for traces to prove it wasn't all a dream, that it's not just a nightmare that recurs night after night. But there's no evidence or she doesn't know where to find it and she goes on that way, full of doubt, always suspecting, in a state of permanent fearfulness.

The house, the smell of the closed-up space, the heavy odor you can smell even from outside, gets in your clothing and your hair: a chronic inescapable foulness. "You stink," her grandmother would say when her father took her to visit once in a while on a Sunday, only very occasionally. Her large black grandmother would heat water and scrub her body with a bundle of herbs until her skin burned. She'd rub her with talcum and cologne, trim her finger and toenails, dress her in her cousin's bathrobes, and sit her on the doorstep for the rest of the afternoon. The cousins beside her played with dolls in elegant outfits or with miniature kitchen sets or with coloring books and magic markers and they'd ignore her. She ignored them, too, not out of indifference or pride, but out of fear.

Only as she returned to her street was the little girl aware of the stench of her home; she'd recognize it from out in the hallway before she opened the door, a bitter wave of smell, then she'd get used to it again.

The mother sleeps late and the child gets up cautiously and slips over into the corner where she has her kingdom: bits of paper, some pencil stubs, empty matchboxes she makes into furniture for her paper dolls. She has a large paper family, ever growing and more united: they marry, have children and grandchildren, and they're very happy. They're a little like her own family, like her mother, who is the Mom, and her father, who is Dad, and a Grandma and Cousins, who are all charming and affectionate. She spends a lot of time with her paper family; she gets to know them better and better and care more about them. They keep seeming more real to her, as if they were replacing the everyday world, taking on an existence of their own, forming a solid family circle, in a secure and loving space.

When her mother wakes up, she gives her milk and bread, and goes off. Her fear looms larger: it's in the humid pattern of the fogged walls and in the shrieks of the crazy man on the floor below and in the spider webs hanging from the ceiling. The child and all her paper relatives hide from fear in the bathroom that has the only window that opens out onto the street; there's a little light there, a breath of air, and the noises of the outside world can be heard there: sounds that don't frighten.

Sometimes her mother stays. She makes her move around from one place to another. She always seems to be right behind the child as if on purpose, while she tries to put their home in order. She scrubs and shakes the rugs, swirling the dust and stirring up the cockroaches. The little girl watches her, seeing her tired sweaty face and her mouth twisted into an exasperated expression. Then she sees her give up, sees her abandon the whole huge, useless, sporadic effort.

Her mother weeps, lying in the bed, covering her face with both her hands. Her mother cries and swears through her fingers, her shoulders shaking. Her voice is high pitched and grating. The child watches her from her corner, her eyes huge and unblinking, without tears. She never cries, not even when she sees her mother weeping and she's afraid she's going to die, that she's already died, that nothing more can happen after that. But it goes on, it's prolonged for an eternity, for longer than an eternity. The child drifts off and at some point she falls asleep. When her mother, tired of weeping, lifts her head and sees the little girl sleeping, she shakes her and wakes her up. She tells her she's hard hearted, that she doesn't love her mother, that she should hug and kiss her. Then the child realizes that it wasn't death that was happening. With passive resignation she puts her arms around her mother's neck and waits for everything to finally be over in order to finally, finally die.

Her paper Mom only cries from happiness. The child cries from happiness, too, sometimes, when she hugs her paper Mom. They hug each other and say loving things to each other. Then the paper Dad comes and takes them to Grandma's house. Paper Grandma has fixed lunch for them, all the child's favorite foods. The paper cousins play with the little girl on the doorstep. The little girl has lots of dolls and she loans them to her cousins. She loans them her bathrobes, too; she has lots of bathrobes, one in every color, and the cousins tell her she's the best cousin in the world, that they love her a lot, really a lot, and they hope she comes back soon. Grandma kisses her on both cheeks and tells her she is her favorite granddaughter, and gives her a bag of caramels for the trip home. The child returns home with her paper parents. She takes a bath, puts on violet perfume, and climbs into a bed that is her very own bed, all her own. Paper Mom pulls up the covers and tells her a story about princesses, and paper Dad plays the guitar and sings her a song. Mom and Dad kiss each other, smiling, then they lean down and kiss the little girl. They wait until she falls asleep, then they tiptoe over to their big bed.

Sometimes the paper family gets worn out with so much hugging. Sometimes they get tears in their necks, the weakest part of them, and the little girl has to make new ones. She draws great big eyes on them and smiling mouths. Every time someone gets torn, she makes a new one, but she never throws the old ones away. She puts them away in the shoebox where she keeps her treasures. She has lots and lots of old paper family members in there. The one she has most of is Mom, because she has hugged her so much. There's nothing better than hugging paper Mom while they say loving things to each other.

One day, in one of her spasmodic housekeeping attacks, her mother grabbed the shoebox that held the child's treasures and emptied it into the trash bag where she was stuffing the garbage and litter that had accumulated in the corners. In a single instant the child saw everything disappear: her drawings, her matchbox furniture, the two-color pencil her father had given her, and her entire paper family. She didn't react, or make any sound at all, not a single complaint or lament; she just mentally re-lived—over and over again—her mother's gesture as she tossed her treasures into the bag. Her mother kept on moving randomly around the room, picking things up, straightening things, but the child no longer sees her mother, she only sees the odious person who has deprived her of her world. She feels more horror than she ever has before, a painful horror that impedes her breathing, clouds her vision, makes her arms and legs tremble. She keeps watch on the odious person, studies each one of her movements, waits quietly until she comes close and leans over to pick something up off the floor; her neck is close, her exposed, fragile neck, and in a single animal leap the child fastens her teeth onto that neck, bites down hard, blindly resisting the jerking and tugging, the contortions, the blows of the person who is trying to pull her off, but is unable to. The child pours all of her energy into that bite, all the stored up energy of her resentment and her deprivation, her fears and her love.

They fall together, for the first time really together, child and mother, for the first time in their lives the two of them united—in that gushing of blood and that unending stench—in a true embrace.

Translation by Mary G. Berg

Waiting

Ronaldo Menéndez Plasencia

"You're the Chief, eh? No offense, but around these parts, Chiefs
have faces showing the years they've been on the job. I hope you
don't take this the wrong way, but I wasn't expecting a kid fresh
out of the Academy, like you guys say. I met one a long while back,
which was the only time I set foot out of Los Hoyos and that was
because no Chief ever made it here. That one had a thin mustache,
like you, but he didn't have your build and he had lots of years
etched on his face. He also had an unexceptional scar halfway down
his cheek. Sorry if I'm beating around the bush, but I don't like
getting down to brass tacks right off because that confuses people
and keeps them from seeing eye to eye. Understanding between
two individuals starts to spark halfway through a good bottle of
rum, so tell those two men at the entrance, which isn't really an
entrance because nobody but me will be coming through it, to go
fetch us some more rum since this is going to stretch out for most
of the night. To be honest, I'm nothing but an informer and so as
not to have that make me feel bad, I'd like you to treat me like a
guest and not like one of your workers, if you get my drift. Like a
guest who's about to tell you quite a story, which is the excuse for
not wasting this bottle of rum.

You came to Los Hoyos to investigate a death under your charge.
But you do know you're not on your turf. How else can I put it? You
really don't know the people here or the lay of the land. And the land
doesn't matter, because I, who's never really traveled, picture the
planet as just miles and miles of grass and hills, with the sun and
moon shining above it all. I know some travelers, and they tell me
that people are people everywhere. Sure, names change, but people
are people and names are names and the difference between *man*
and *pan* is one measly letter. Your father was a Chief, from the old
school, and though you're fresh out of the Academy, you know I'm
right. You say that years ago, your father was investigating another
murder under his charge that dead-ended here in Los Hoyos. Whatever comes from there to here seems to disappear. Your father never
solved the case, so now I've got to hand it over to you even though
you're fresh out of the Academy and your father didn't have the nerve
to go into Los Hoyos. Who knows, maybe it was fate for you to become
Chief, from the old school, and for me to turn informer.

So I'll tell you about your father's dead man, who was never really
dead and what happened to your dead man, who really is dead; you

saw for yourself when they dug him up with a hole through the forehead.

Years ago, *El Negro,* your dad's dead man—a pussycat who thought he was a tiger because he could shoot straight—came into these parts. He had two friends from around here that were good and dead, even back then. That's lesson #1. Let me explain. The three of them got together and went into the gorges. No matter how loud you scream there, no one'll hear you not because of the distance, but because the land dips and forms walls. That's how it started . . . Put down your glass now; this booze's having such a good time it doesn't give a shit about us. Well, our little pussycats went way down in the gorges and as luck would have it, they found a boy all by himself. God knows what that kid was doing there; maybe he didn't mind being in the gorges alone. These three decided to grab him up—maybe because youngsters around here think they're all so smart. I won't bore you with details anyone can imagine, but not one person saw how it all started. Hold on, I'll explain. They fucking tortured him, did whatever pigs do to make themselves feel superior. But they went way too far. Someone who shouldn't have seen the rape saw it—another of those odd twists of fate. After all, this is a story of coincidences. Like you and me sitting here with a bottle of rum between us, you solving a crime and me snitching. Understand? I believe there's a reason for everything. Hmmm. Do you know *El Viejo*? He owns the ranch where they found your dead person. Do you know why they call him *El Viejo*? Back then he wasn't old, he had a regular name with a Mr. in front and a whole life ahead of him. He was a widower whose wife had died giving birth to their only child, the boy the three troublemakers ended up sodomizing. And it wasn't a coincidence that there was a witness. Without getting off his horse, this sharpshooter dropped someone who a second earlier had been jumping around and laughing. With a mocking laugh turned frozen, he sent him to his death. The second shot made the horse jump a foot, or maybe sheer rage clouded *El Viejo's* eyesight. But he missed the assailants and killed his own son. A hole right through the neck. *El Negro* hightailed it out of there and hid in the brush. The other assailant stood over the stiffening body, not knowing what had happened, till he was pulled up by the hair and stretched out flat. *El Viejo* didn't kill him right off, which would've been better. Instead, he pulled out a shearing knife, the kind that glints from side to side. The man who lost his son went crazy. Believe me when I say he used him as bait to get *El Negro* to fight. But *El Negro* wouldn't show his face. Since *El Viejo* lacked imagination, his torture consisted of slicing the skin along the fingers, all the way down to the wrists, and then shooting off the hands. Everyone says this was the only time a scream escaped the gorges. *El Negro* was reputed to be a good shot, but panic must have overtaken him in the brush because he missed. *El Negro* actually aimed for *El Viejo*'s chest but hit him in the shoulder instead. And then he scampered off. The wounded father finished off the others, calmly got back on his horse, which surely gave him an advantage, and chased after him. But *El Negro* had the devil running wild inside and when he finally made it back home, without getting hurt, he came face-to-face with that Domingo Suárez, who twenty years ago was waiting there with his saddled horse. Not asking but not really stealing, *El Negro* just mounted the horse and disappeared. *El Viejo* never caught up to him. That's it, Chief, the story of your father's dead man; now you know he never died, but disappeared terrified.

There's just a drop of rum left so I better cut this short. Everyone in Los Hoyos knows and remembers this tragedy. We buried his son and burned the others so your father, the Chief, wouldn't find any clues. Oddly, *El Viejo*'s hair turned gray over night. Sure as you're looking at his white hair that's exactly what he looked like after burying his son. That's why they call him *El Viejo* and everyone is scared shit- less of him. He spent a month looking high and low for *El Negro*. He didn't find him and he went nuts: he couldn't believe that *El Negro* had escaped. *El Viejo* suspected that he had never left Los Hoyos and that one of us was hiding him. That's why he's sniffed around here these past twenty years waiting for him to reappear . . . One last drink, Chief, 'cause here comes the hole-in-the-head dead guy you dug up this afternoon, the one named Domingo Suárez. I'm sure you can finish the story. I'm told that Academy-types are pretty good at constructing stories. For some reason, Domingo Suárez decided to come back to Los Hoyos yesterday morning. Do you know what he did? Out of pity or fate or because he couldn't resist the urge of telling what he thought the other person wanted, he went straight to *El Viejo* and told him how the story ended, how a frightened *El Negro* lost himself in the brush. Imagine, *El Viejo* took out his gun and put a hole in Suárez's head—a beauty mark—right above his eyes.

We're out of rum, Chief. There's Domingo Suárez's body; he thought that *El Viejo* needed a tiny bit of truth. And, Chief: do you know why I'm here snitching? *El Viejo* asked me to, saying there's no point waiting any longer. So put a rush on it, Chief, shoot him first thing in the morning. It'll give him some pleasure."

Translation by David Unger

When Life Gives You Lemons

Mirta Yáñez

My blood still boils when I think about it. Seems like it was only yesterday. There's no word for what this girl had to go through back then. You couldn't make me return to that life, even if you held a gun to my head. And don't give me that crap that I'm brainwashing you. That's not it at all. You see, I've learned a thing or two in my time. So now you're going to hear everything, from A to Z. Those stories are stuck in a corner of my brain and no matter how much I try to forget them, they come out for a little stroll once in a while. When I'm done talking, you'll be so worked up we'll have to swab your forehead with alcohol to cool you off. But that's how it is. When certain things happen in a woman's life, she decides it's better to keep it under wraps than to spread the details all over town, spoiling everybody's day. Who hasn't been through something that weighs you down over the years. You'd rather walk in front of a train than talk about it. So why do you want to drag this nonsense out of me now? Sure, you've just told me how you're leaving the country and how you plan to whore yourself to survive up there. And with a tongue looser than shit, you've reminded me that until just the other day (as they say) I was a whore, though now I'm trying to pass myself off as a decent woman. So I'm going to tell you even if I have to haul you to the emergency room afterwards. At first, I wasn't one of those girls who had nothing better to do than hang out with low-lifes. I was the cream of the crop, all things considered. My old man, may he rest in peace, well, sure, he was knotted up inside by what he had to give up and the anger he must have felt for so long, but he taught me to read and to write with neat Palmer-method penmanship. Before misfortune came around our house with my old man's illness and my brother Quique's death up north, I considered myself a well-brought up young lady, and I even spoke a bit of broken English with some Swahili thrown in for good measure. So, when I first started living that wicked life, I was a stuck up, classy girl. Not for the average Joe. And boy did a girl have to get thick-skinned about the things she had to do! I even felt superior to those other girls who had to walk the streets, when I was set up in a place that was all neat and clean, where they treated me like a queen.

And when a *mister* came calling, I never doubted he'd ask for me. I'd even come home with some new English word I'd picked up and repeat it—not knowing what it meant. My old man sitting there in his arm chair would blow a gasket and turn blue in the face because he'd been a waiter in Texas and he knew a thing or two. Even though I was the one who brought home the bacon, many times I had to stroke the old man's ego and butter up Mama so she wouldn't start to cry. I'd say that better times were coming. Better times. What a crock! To this day when I remember what happened I don't know whether to cry or what. They say misfortunes file in like ants. First it was my brother Quique: out of the blue a letter arrived telling Mama, "Damn it, I'm dying," and then came a postcard from I don't know who, telling us he was dead and buried in a town whose name I can't remember. Then Papa gets sick and loses his job; Mama with her bad heart and me having to start a new line of work. At least we had enough to get by, pay the rent for our tenement room, and buy food every day. Then one fine day everything really fell apart. Every blessed thing. The police came and had a row with Sra. Obdulia, the storefront madam. Murderers: on Sundays, strolling in fine linen suits, their wives on their arms. Then when they patrolled the neighborhood, they'd steal our money in broad daylight. And if Mrs. Obdulia didn't pay right on time, they'd cut our kite strings. Don't get me started on that! On the very same day, I found myself out of a steady job and lost my old man. Back home in our lousy tenement room with the bad news, I couldn't get the words out because I ran smack into Mama. She was hugging Papa who'd just keeled over, deader than a doornail, coffee cup still in his hand. And he hadn't spilled a drop, ladies and gentlemen. Our last dime flew out of our hands for the wake and to dress the old guy in decent clothes. By the day of the funeral, he was so stiff it was a royal pain to get a guayabera shirt on him. We never did get it on right. But finally it was over and Mama was satisfied. I said to myself: what now, dear Mother Mary. I had no choice but to pound the pavement and see what it was like to wait in the cold and rain, hoping to reel in some customer, ready to latch on to anyone who came along. I'd strut my stuff, but no one came. I'd go back to our miserable room empty-handed and Mama would look at me like a lamb with its head cut off because she hadn't had a hot meal in a week. We considered those burgers they sold on the corner a real feast. As for me, it'd been three days since I'd eaten anything at all. I'd buy Mama a burger and hand her the line that I'd eaten mine on the way home. The half a block I had to walk from the burger stand to the tenement was torture. I'd look at the burger in my hand and tell myself she wouldn't notice a little bite and if she did, I'd say they sold it to me that way. I'd pinch crumbs off the edge of the bread and put them in my mouth. That only made it worse. By the time I got home I could've eaten a whole cow if they'd put one in front of me. I gave Mama that measly burger and washed my hands in the wash basin in the hall because just a whiff of that greasy little thing made my stomach turn somersaults. I felt like I was going to faint right then and there. So that's how I headed off to work all those nights during hurricane season. I had so few customers, and there was no end in sight to that hunger. On the eighth night this dolled-up old broad parked her long-finned Caddie at the corner where I was showing off my wares, stuck her head out the window and looked me up and down. "I sure don't need thie aggravation," I said to myself, and turned my back and pretended to be looking at the mannequins in a store window on Virtudes Street, keeping an eye on that old bag to see if she'd left. But after a while, something told me to look over my shoulder and there's that woman, who'd seen better days, she must have been at least eighty years old, covered in gaudy jewelry, her head cocked, looking at me like I was some monkey in the zoo. "It's my son!" she blurted out, as if she wanted to close the deal fast. I kept my mouth shut; to tell the truth I didn't know what to say. Next thing I knew, she was pulling me very slowly toward her Caddie. I got in without a second thought, already plotting what I'd do with the money. Sure, it was a strange situation: a hi-toned lady out at eleven o'clock at night looking for a girl like me for her son, but, at the crossroads of life, your thoughts take off like a rocket and I couldn't quit thinking about the feast we'd have the next day. So I said, "OK," and went with the old girl. At first she didn't even look at me, but after a bit she took out a large bill and looked me straight in the eye. Sizing me up. There was something fishy about the way she said, "twenty now and twenty *later,*" just like in the American movies when the gangster gets sent on a difficult job. Maybe it was the way she said *later* or maybe it was how much she offered me. You felt like a millionaire with that kind of money in those days. The thing is, I got a knot in my throat, but I told myself don't be a shithead, take advantage of your good luck, a chance like this only comes along once in a lifetime. My head was in that tug of war as the Caddie slipped through an iron gate covered with huge, blood-red hibiscus. I thought I must be uptown, in Miramar. I've tried to find the place again so many times with no luck. Sometimes, in the Cerro neighborhood I'd tell myself, "This is it." But no. I walk around the Vedado district, with all its mansions, and the thought, "Here it is," pops into my head. But I'm wrong again. There's no other gate like that one, with the bedraggled hibiscus hanging from its iron fangs. It's as if the earth had swallowed it up. When the old lady parked the car and told me not to make any noise so I wouldn't wake the servants, I was completely freaked out. If I'd pinched myself hard to see if this was a nightmare, I'd have left a huge, bloody black mark. We crossed a kitchen five times bigger than our room in the tenement. On the table they'd left a covered glass bowl filled with chicken and rice, and my eyes went straight to it. The old lady noticed and repeated, *"Later."* When I heard her say that again, I looked down and saw a crisp twenty peso bill in my hand, a sight I hadn't seen for a long time. It smelled wonderful. I tucked it safely away and told myself, come what may, that bill's already in the bank. Just in case. It felt like a thorn sticking in me. As we were climbing the stairs, the old woman seemed to want to tell me something. I was so cocky that I said, "So what's the deal?" She looked at me and didn't say a word. I felt like a rag, only good for mopping the floor. That's when I started to look around for an escape route in case the deal went bad. Right then, we stopped in front of a door that was propped half open, and the old woman spoke to me. Her words are stuck in my brain. I'll take them with me to the grave. As if I were a stray dog, she said to me, "Behave yourself, my son is very special." *Very special.* That phrase still haunts me. It makes my blood boil and I feel like I'm about to explode. I went into the bedroom and know what I saw? On the bed was a kind of pasty-white creature, with a sheet pulled up to its chest. Unshaven. At first glance I didn't catch on, but then I saw the guy's big hands flapping around, slobber running down his chin and heard grunts coming from his throat. I shouted, "But señora, he's a freak!" She looked at me with eyes hard as dog's teeth, and answered, "I'll pay." And I remembered the new bill, and the other twenty she owed me, and Mama back in our room with her bad heart, and the three months' rent we owed. Even the chicken and rice popped into my head, because now I was thinking rapid fire, like a machine gun. I saw that bowl growing, blowing up like a balloon there in the kitchen, rice spilling out from under the lid, the voice of the radio announcer back in our room in the tenements, our room overflowing with chicken and rice and that damned jingle for *Jon Chi Rice, big plump kernels. Jon Chi Rice, bursting with flavor. Jon Chi Rice, You're gonna love it.* And I looked down at that fat slob and felt that knot again. This time it sunk to my stomach, then rose to my throat. Despite all that, I told the old bag I was OK. When life gives you lemons . . . Just as the lady was about to leave the room, that knot slid down my chest and I think it nicked my heart. I crumpled to the floor. That must've caused an uproar in the house, because the old lady thought I'd died. And I think I did die a little. When I came to in the Caddie, the man driving said he was the chauffeur and that all the racket had wakened everyone in the mansion, that the lady ordered me to forget the whole thing, and that the twenty pesos were mine if I kept my lips zipped. She told him to take me to the hospital. And I said to him, "Over my dead body. Do me a favor, pal, let me off at the next bus stop." I got out of that Caddie as fast as the devil carries off a soul.

But why are you looking at me like that? Don't make that face. You look like you're about to croak. You don't think your mother's telling you lies, do you?

Translation by Pamela Carmell

Black and White*

Aida Bahr

Rebecca's daughter

I don't know whether to think you're a saint or a fool, Luisa, although maybe they're the same thing. Did Rebecca's phone call really upset you so much that you had to go hide? The living room smells like death. How long is it since anybody's been here? Even the mailman knows to come to the back door. You've created a boundary, an invisible line that says that the house starts at the dining room. It's probably so you can imagine Rebecca still here and Leon still alive. And if you keep the lights turned off, it must be because darkness allows you to imagine furniture and curtains that haven't been here for years. And it's all a shame, Luisa, because now this house belongs to *you*. Rebecca's not here to tell you what to do. She's lost her rights—if she ever had any—when she left. And it's pathetic to hear you cry talking to her on the phone. Don't give me that "she was crying too" bit since we both know what her tears are worth. Remember how weepy she got when they came to inventory her things before she left and they seized the wedding photo? "Oh, no, not that," she said with rivers gushing from her eyes. So they gave it back to her but she didn't take it after all because without the elegant frame it wasn't the same. If it wasn't going to take center stage on a coffee table where everyone could admire the pearls, fancy beadwork, and intricate lace of her wedding dress, it didn't have the same appeal. You're the only one who believes she got choked up just talking to you. She didn't call to find out about you, Luisa; she still wants to order you around. For her, you've never been more than a servant.

Luisa

That's not true. Rebecca and I are more like sisters than cousins. She and I are the only descendents of the Ricardo family because Mama and Aunt Amalia, even though they got married young, didn't have us until they were in their forties—Mama because she

---

*A conversation between Luisa and her cousin Rebecca's daughter; in essence a way to contrast those who left after the 1959 Revolution and those who stayed. The two narrators alternate in telling about Rebecca, and, through her, the story of a Cuban family.

would always lose the baby in the third or fourth month and Auntie Amalia because she never got pregnant. At age forty Aunt Amalia had Rebecca and the next year I was born, as if Mama had been waiting for a signal. Rebecca and I were always together. They even dressed us alike, except that on Rebecca the clothes looked beautiful while on me they seemed to be hanging from a hook. I turned out like Papa: tall, thin, and gangly. I don't think Mama ever forgave me. Sometimes she looked at me as if my very existence was punishment for some unknown sin. We never really got along. Mama tried her best to mold me and she used to say: "Even though you're younger than Rebecca, you don't always have to do things her way. Sometimes you should be in charge. Tell her you want to play with dolls instead of playing doctor." I tried that, but it always turned out that when Rebecca wanted to play with dolls, or felt like playing nurses, she made it so interesting that I agreed with her. That's just the way it was. At some point Mama got tired of trying to change me. Perhaps it was after father died and we were in mourning, I for a year and she in perpetuity. Neither her body nor her soul ever really gave up mourning. It even offended her that I got to the point of being able to laugh again. That was the worst period of my life because I discovered I could never fill the emptiness that my father's death had left. Rebecca was my salvation. Every time she went out she came by for me and begged so much that mother ended up letting me go with her. Thanks to Rebecca, I went to parties, saw friends, and took walks. If it had been up to mother, I would never have seen a single movie. And was it Rebecca's fault that she was pretty and cheerful while I was unattractive and withdrawn? Anyway, I never felt ill will or jealousy because people preferred her. On the contrary, I had fun because of her romances and many times I helped her arrange to be alone with a boy. Nothing serious happened until Leon appeared, and then it was clear that he was something different. He was twelve years older than Rebecca and was a respected physician. Even before the engagement she paid him special attention, and wouldn't dance with anybody else. I was the beneficiary of her single-mindedness—when boys asked her to dance and she said no, they turned to me. But none of them interested me, and after Leon asked for Rebecca's hand, no one dared to approach us. I didn't really miss the male companionship. Leon was so kind that he never made me feel like a chaperone, or someone extra. It was marvelous. Something in his way of looking at you made you feel protected, safe from everything. He treated us like little girls and brought presents for both of us. He was crazy about Rebecca: when she spoke he smiled, and you could tell that he was not just listening but also looking, drinking her in with his eyes. With me, it was what I said that mattered. Leon and I always found it easy to talk to each other. One afternoon we were discussing a biography of Marie Antoinette by Stefan Zweig, a book Leon had given us and that I, as usual, had read and then summarized for Rebecca. The conversation was about more than an aristocrat facing the guillotine. It was about whether the punishment was fair or not. Rebecca saw Marie Antoinette as a young girl who had done nothing more than amuse herself and said it wasn't reasonable to expect more of someone who became a queen at age sixteen. I argued that Marie Antoinette was a grown woman at the time of the French Revolution and that by then she should have gained some degree of maturity. Zweig (for his part) seemed to me to be enamored of the idea of a beautiful queen meeting a tragic end. To all of this, Leon smiled. He praised my intelligence and said I had common sense, which was rare: "We'll have to take care of you, you're the sort of woman who's becoming extinct." Rebecca thought he was making fun of me and scolded him, but I took it all seriously. Their courtship period was a beautiful, harmonious interlude, but it didn't last long. The wedding was a big deal, first the ceremony in the church and then the festivities. Mama didn't want to go but Aunt Amalia interceded for me and we went for about an hour, enough time to see them cut the cake, sip the cider and kiss. On the way back I cried, but mother didn't even pay attention. At the time, she was already sick but didn't know how serious it was. In any event it didn't matter to her. During Rebecca's honeymoon—days when I never left the house—I realized that mother was going to die. One night while we were eating I asked her if I shouldn't study typing. "Don't be ridiculous," she said, "you have your pension and the house." Mother faded little by little without complaining. The last thing she said was, "I'm coming to join you, Antonio." Not a word for me. I, who cry about everything, was dry-eyed, and empty. It hardly seemed that mother had died but rather that she'd left me alone on purpose. At the funeral itself, Aunt Amalia asked me to come live with her. I said no, and it took Leon's help to convince her to let me go home by myself after the burial. I went to sleep and slept like a rock until the next morning. In the morning Aunt Amalia came back to try to convince me, and I told her I would think about it, and when she left I said to myself: "I've got things to do," and I set to cleaning. I washed doors and windows, swept the roof, and scrubbed the floors. People came to give me their condolences and they couldn't even step inside the door because of all the water from my scrubbing. Rebecca came in the afternoon and found me scouring the cement steps that led to the patio. She completely forgot to mention mother. She sat in the kitchen, and I offered to fix her coffee, but she wouldn't let me. "You're coming with us," she said. And it was just like when we played as children: I knew that she was right.

You were born with a silver spoon in your mouth, as might be expected of Rebecca's daughter. Pretty as a picture. Your grandmother Amalia used to say: she'll be a fashion model. Rebecca dressed you up in such frilly and beautiful outfits that you looked like a princess, and even people who didn't know you felt like they had to pay compliments. One time they gave you three polished, jet-black *azabache* pendants out of fear of the evil eye. And in one of the carnivals they dressed you up as a harem girl and painted your face. They had you ride right on the hood of the car. You surely remember that because it was the happiest moment of your childhood. Three years old. And there you were: a precious little doll seated on top of the hood throwing streamers and kisses.

Rebecca's daughter

The earliest thing I remember are the bars of my cradle. I played that I was a lion in a cage. I crawled and roared. I also remember that the only one who listened to my stories was Leon. He listened attentively and discussed them with me seriously. Rebecca insisted that if I kept it up I'd end up telling lies. I'll never understand her. The day that I ran away from home, the only thing she did was to laugh at the sight of me with high heels, jewelry, and makeup. They found me three blocks away from home. I hadn't yet started school, so I must have been less than five years old. I suppose that in those days I was happy, but I can't remember that happiness, just a few good moments that fell my way like the aces from a deck of cards. One of my best memories is of an afternoon on the patio when I was alone, seated on the ground with a plate heaped with caramels. Other good memories are when Uncle Pedro taught me to play cards in the middle of hurricane Flora; well, I know it wasn't exactly a hurricane because he never left the farm, but still it was raining really hard that afternoon. He also taught me to ride horseback and drink sugar cane juice. The farm was a paradise, but we didn't get to go very often . . . Rebecca always complained about how far it was, how bad the road was, about the mud and the insects—about everything. When she wasn't around Leon, she was disparaging of Uncle Pedro, who was such a macho guy that he and Leon hardly seemed like brothers. But guess who always came to our rescue. The trips to the farm are among my happiest memories. Another time was when Grandma Amalia and Grandpa Enrique went north, their kisses wet with tears as they said goodbye. Of the trip to Havana, the one where they said they took me to the city's Coney Island Amusement Park, I don't remember anything. Oh, and of course there was the beach. Rebecca would lie in the sun wearing her Hawaiian pareu while Leon taught me how to swim. One day we couldn't go in because the sea was so rough and the waves so furious that they could drag down a grown man. While we were sitting on the beach, a bent over old man with white hair walked by. He was all by himself. He didn't dare go in the water but he got close enough to splash a little water on himself when the waves came in. But then he got knocked down by a big wave and the poor old man had to retreat. I felt sad seeing him so unhappy and defenseless. It made me angry that he wanted to bathe in the ocean and the sea wouldn't allow it, just like if someone came to knock on your door to ask you for something and you threw the person out. Alms. Oh yes, the question of charity. That's something for which I'll never forgive Rebecca. I used to save coins to give them to the old people who sat in the doors of the church. I'd go to nine o'clock mass so I could sleep in the morning. After I had my first communion, they let me go to seven o'clock mass and I didn't see any more beggars. But, before, when I used to go with Rebecca, I did see them. There were three old men. I would go up to them and give them my coins, two or three to each one, and they would smile and say thank you and God bless you. Rebecca never gave them anything. I went up to them all by myself, a good little girl giving alms. One morning there was a younger woman there and when she saw the three coins she threw them on the ground. I was shocked because she said "shit," just like that, "shit," and then Rebecca came and rescued me while the woman said, "Money, what I need is money—not these shitty coins." The old men had never protested. Rebecca said they must be millionaires with all the alms they got at every mass. And I was giving them coins. I'll never be able to forgive or forget that incident. I was just a little girl and I didn't understand, and Rebecca in her own way helped me to understand.

If you don't want this letter from Rebecca to end up in the bathroom wastebasket, don't leave it out where it can be seen. After all, you're the one who wants to know how she's doing. And you needn't make an effort to tell us that she still hasn't found work and that she's living with Bonnie and not Carmela. Everything that the letter says we already know; there's never any mystery with Rebecca. It's was obvious that she wasn't going to stay with Carmela after Pedro kicked her out. Carmela is cheap and Rebecca likes luxury. Didn't you say that Bonnie has money? Leon's inconsolable widow won't be looking for work. She's not like you, Luisa, almost going crazy and asking God to help you get ahead. Now, there's nothing left for you to sell. Well, yes, there are the hidden jewels, Rebecca's famous emeralds that matched her eyes. You looked almost comical when you said you'd rather work like a slave than sell them. But you'll have to do something. Yesterday you cried after refusing the chickens that Manuel brought and nobody knew if you cried because there wasn't any meat in the house or because you couldn't believe that Manuel wanted you to pay. And what did you expect, that he's going to just give them to you because Pedro was always kind to him? In any event, Manuel was working for a salary, and if he was Pedro's friend, something no one can prove, you're really nothing more than the cousin of the wife of the brother of his friend. That's a pretty distant relationship, don't you think? And the fact that Pedro's niece is in the middle of it all hardly matters either. You should be thankful that he is bringing you things, because many people would have to go to him to buy them. You also have to remember that if he keeps coming in vain, he's going to stop coming. But don't worry; you have rice and beans and there's meat once a week. Isn't that right? So be happy.

Luisa

Ever since '59 everything's been falling apart back there. Well, maybe since '60, because in '59 there was all the rejoicing over the triumph of the revolution. Leon laughed because he said that all of a sudden we discovered that everything was linked to the date July 26, and how could you explain that Batista had lasted so long.* From '59 I just remember one bad thing; that's when Bonnie, Rebecca's best friend, went North. While Bonnie was here, Carmela was nothing more than an acquaintance. Bonnie was nice and spoke a kind of comical Spanish. She used to say: I am (soy) really confused, I am (estoy) clumsy in Spanish, getting our two ways of expressing "to be" completely mixed up. She could never understand the difference between "ser" and "estar." Her family had extensive holdings, and they left sometime between May and June of 1959, while we were still in the period of euphoria. Later everyone said that they had had foresight. First because of the hassles about ownership and then because of military conscription. Rebecca's friends kept leaving until only Carmela Aguirre was left. Aunt Amalia and Uncle Enrique left shortly after the money was changed. They had theirs all hidden away in the house and they were ruined. They tried to convince Leon to go, too, but he had lived in New York before he got married and had no desire to return He did, however, give them a blank check so that they could use money he had left in a bank there. That money ended up being a big help because six months after they got there Uncle Enrique suffered a heart attack and couldn't work

---

*July 26th—After the 1959 revolution, much was made of the date July 26 to commemorate the July 26, 1953 attack by Fidel Castro and his followers on the Moncada Barracks in Santiago. A Cuban song includes the refrain: "For us, it's always the 26th."

anymore. Even now they're still living on welfare, which is why
Rebecca couldn't stay with them. Another person who suffered a lot
was Pedro. The second agrarian reform law took away almost all
of his farm—the best land according to him—and he became bitter
and left. When he came to say goodbye and bent down to kiss me,
I realized that his hair had turned white. That's how we ended up
being alone. Pedro prospered in the U.S. and offered to help us come
whenever we wanted. From the very first, Rebecca wanted to go.
Every time a letter from Pedro arrived she argued with Leon about
it. In May of '67 she insisted for the last time. I can remember it
vividly: Leon seated in the rocking chair and she on the footstool to
the side, leaning on his knees and begging. His response had always
been that he wasn't missing out on anything. This time he said:
"Here I have a name and I'm respected." "You can make a name for
yourself there as well," she said. But looking at her with sadness
he replied: "Not now," and she understood and ran to the bedroom
with tears in her eyes. They didn't speak of it again, not even when
Carmela herself planned to leave. I'm not sure why it took so long
for Rebecca to realize about Leon's health; perhaps she wanted to
hide from reality and stick her head in the ground like an ostrich.
I understood from the very beginning. When Leon had to work at
night I was the one who stayed up to heat his meal and talk to
him. One day the hospital called to say he was doing an emergency
operation and would get home late. When he arrived it was after
midnight and he was not in his own car. They brought him home.
When I went out into the hallway, it scared me half to death to see
him; he had to lean against the wall to be able to walk and seemed a
shadow of himself. I helped him sit down. What's the matter? What
happened? I asked. No answer. I asked him if I should bring him
some food and he nodded no with his head and just stayed seated,
leaning back, with his eyes closed. He was breathing so weakly that
I could hardly hear him. I'll call Rebecca, I said, but he took my hand
in his. What is it, Leon? What happened? He spoke with long pauses,
as if he didn't have sufficient breath for a whole sentence. "There was
an accident. In the middle of the operation the man's heart stopped.
I couldn't pull him out of it. I couldn't." I tried to console Leon: I'm
sure you did everything you could. He closed his eyes again and
said simply: "The patient died and I'm alive." And it was then that
I realized that Leon had suffered a heart attack at the very time he
was fighting to save another man's life. He hadn't been able to go on.
No doubt they tended to Leon more than the other man, so he felt
guilty for having stolen another man's chance to live. The remorse
of that incident devastated him as much as his own illness. He was
never the same after that. When he tried to tell a joke, he ended up
wanting to bite his tongue with regret for having spoken. It was then

that the really bad years began. 1968 was the worst. We lost Leon, which meant losing everything; it was the greatest sorrow of my life. When Papa died I was just a little girl; then when Mama died the sensation was very different. When Leon died my world came apart, and I couldn't even cry because someone had to look after the house and Rebecca had to be sedated three times during the wake and couldn't make it to the burial. The next few days we were like ghosts in the house. Carmela came every day. I left her alone with Rebecca so I could take care of the household chores and could cry alone in the kitchen. If I had money for all the tears I spilled in that kitchen, I'd never be hungry. One month after Leon died, we went to take flowers to the cemetery. There at Leon's tomb Rebecca told me that she was going to seek permission to leave. I looked at her without knowing what to say and she explained: Mother will take care of the legal matters and Pedro will give us the money. You're coming with us aren't you? No, I said. The people I love are buried here and I'm staying here with them.

You must remember about all of that. It wasn't when you were really young. I'm sure you remember because it was the time you began to change. You went from being a sweet, outgoing, talkative little girl to becoming a silent and withdrawn human being. Everyday you hid a bit more of yourself. Rebecca always tried to get you to go out with her, and you always said no until at last she gave up and began to go out by herself. The more you refused to talk, the more she talked. Couldn't you see that she was about to go crazy? The culmination came when it was time for Carmela to leave. I know it must have been hard for you: the day you turned twelve you didn't even smile when Rebecca woke you up with a kiss and congratulations. This year the nightmare will end, she said, and she was right, except that your nightmare and hers were different. Once the unpleasantness of the pre-departure inventory was over, Rebecca seemed to be humming with happiness. You, on the other hand, seemed to be dying inside. The night you and Rebecca were headed for Varadero you had us worried. You'd never before thrown a plate of food on the floor. Then in the station you sat on the floor and acted deaf when they called, and had to be put on the train. Your eyes had a vacant look as if you weren't going toward Matanzas and from there to Varadero, but rather toward hell. What happened next only you know.

Rebecca's daughter

Torches and smoke. That's my memory of the station. A very long black train seen as if I were looking at it from outside my body: I saw myself seated at the edge of the platform with my legs dangling.

There was a drunk lying on a bench like a bundle of rags. I even thought that I was dead and that my body had been thrown out, but I don't remember much more. Just scenes and sensations. The bathroom of the train wet with puddles and full of paper. The metal door felt cold. I remember how that cold penetrated. The trip made me seasick. The trees ran backwards, and all of a sudden a station would appear: they were always the same: the same fence, the same building, the same benches. The train blew its whistle and lurched forward, and the trees began to run backwards again. I'm not sure how long it took or what Rebecca did. When we got to Matanzas a man in the station was selling Caracas cakes or some kind of bread like that. I asked Rebecca to buy me some but she put me in a rented van where we were all on top of each other and on top of the luggage. The man with Caracas bread remained behind; people were buying, breaking off pieces, and eating. Rebecca tried to give me some of the meat pie she had brought, but I wasn't hungry. In Varadero we stayed in the house of a woman who rented out space to people who were leaving; it was the same place where Carmela had stayed. The woman already knew about Rebecca, greeted her as if they were old friends and even fixed her coffee. They sat in the kitchen and talked for a long time. The woman told Rebecca that they would make her give up her wedding ring because it was gold and suggested that she swallow it. Just pretend it's a pill she said. The house had a wood swing on the porch, and I spent some time there. I suppose that at some point I bathed, we ate, and that they gave us a room to sleep in, but I don't know, I just can't remember. I was on the swing when Rebecca called me to get dressed. I wanted to stay dressed in pants but she made me put on a gingham dress. I closed the suitcase and heard the car honk outside. Hurry up she said. As I left the room I saw her on the sidewalk with the man who was going to take us to the airport, a fat man with a double chin that almost reached his chest. He looked at Rebecca as if he were going to eat her up. They were standing next to each other and their thighs were touching. I didn't think about anything; I didn't know what I was going to do. Instead of walking to the sidewalk I went to the patio. Something snapped inside my head; I saw the zinc fence and jumped over it. Behind the fence was underbrush. I began to run, but at first not very fast. Then I heard shouts and realized that I was escaping, or that I could escape. I ran like crazy through the countryside, falling down and getting up and running again, and when I had to stop I lay down between some rocks and a thorny *marabusal* bush with my throat dry, scared to death like in hide and seek, where you know they are looking for you and that if they find you, you lose. Nightfall came and I stayed put, paralyzed, not daring to move. Suddenly I heard noises and a flashlight beam was on me. Someone pulled me up by the arms. I saw some very blue eyes, thought it was an American, and began to shout that I didn't want to go, that I wanted to stay in Cuba. Then I saw a dark haired man and realized that they were both dressed in olive green. I tried to walk but I couldn't; the one with the blue eyes carried me to a jeep and they took me to a guard post. I heard them talking on the phone and they mentioned Rebecca. I shouted again and grabbed the arm of the official: Don't let her take me, please, don't let her take me. She can't take you because she's already gone, he said. I looked at him stupefied and began to laugh and cry at the same time. They brought me a glass of milk and then I fell asleep and didn't even dream.

Seeing you place flowers on the tomb, dressed in mourning, anyone would think that you were the widow. Leon was a lucky fool. Instead of choosing you he married Rebecca and got you both. An ideal combination: a beautiful lover to show off and a perfect housewife. How could you stand it? Your mother was right to be irritated with you. You could have married, had children, your own house, your own life, but instead you preferred to be a shadow of Rebecca. If you'd wanted to, who knows. After all Leon was closer to you than to her. The way in which he talked to you, looked at you, smiled at you. If you'd wanted to . . .

Luisa

I've been happy. Very happy. Perhaps I've had more than my share of happiness. Life is never black and white, or rather it *is,* but the two colors are mixed: nothing is entirely black or entirely white. All those dances, those strolls in the park, so many lovely memories that can't be separated from Rebecca; thanks to her I enjoyed them. Should I have gotten married? I had some suitors before mother died, but not a single one stirred my interest. If I had stayed in my house perhaps others would have shown interest, and probably not because of me, but because of the advantages of my being a single girl with a house. When I lived with Leon and Rebecca I met many men, friends of Leon, and occasionally one would pay me a compliment or drop a hint. But I never encouraged any of them; I didn't need to. I've lived the life I chose and the bad things that have happened were not anybody's fault in particular. The break-up of the family, Leon's heart attack: Rebecca suffered more from them than I did. She always needed things that weren't of interest to me and she kept losing them one by one. For example, she loved candy and Leon would get it for her two boxes at a time; even more when she was pregnant. She always insisted that I eat one as soon as she opened the box because her craving was so strong that she could eat the whole box in minutes and would then feel sorry that there wasn't one left for me. In some ways her weaknesses were not her fault. She was always spoiled, pampered, and treated like a doll, but she was also sweet, cheerful and good-natured. She simply wasn't prepared to face life on her own. She'd always had someone to do things for her: first Aunt Amalia and Uncle Enrique, then Leon, and at the end just me. If she is living with Bonnie now it's not just for economic reasons. Every time we talk on the phone she ends by telling me: I really miss you. She feels my absence much more than I feel hers. It's always been that way. It was always up to her to give and to me to receive.

You were very sentimental as a little girl; you had a special capacity to enjoy love. You don't remember it, but one time you saw Leon and Rebecca kissing on the lips and you ran out to tell everybody you saw: my mother and father are going to get married. It was the same with the gift of *La Edad de Oro*.* Do you remember that you decided that you would begin to read it on the very day of your birthday and that you've kept it on the night stand unopened until this very day? Leon was sorry because he understood that you would have wanted such a special gift to arrive—not on just any day—but on some important date. At the same time he was proud that you would organize things that way; he said that it was good that you were capable of wishful thinking. Now, on the other hand you've become hard and practical. You're obsessed with all of Rebecca's supposed failings. And now you don't even call her Mama.

Rebecca's daughter

Carmela's house was just like her. From the outside it seemed like a lovely big house, but once you went through the door you found sagging furniture, cobwebs on the lamps, pictures and door-molding and rooms that were empty because she had sold off everything. The first room was full of cardboard boxes, piles of cardboard boxes, who knows for what, and two more rooms that were empty, and then her room which led to the hallway of the patio and the bathroom. Her room did have the bedroom furniture intact. In the patio, grass was growing between the cracks in the cement. The garden wall and the wall of the bathroom were covered with mold and bracken. Apart from the living room, that room and the kitchen, there was no place to sit down. They sent me to the patio and I sat down on the floor of the hallway. I don't know what they were thinking when they told me to amuse myself back there. How did they imagine that an eleven-year-

---

La Edad de Oro (The Golden Age)—famous book of children's literature written by the Cuban national hero, José Martí. It contains stories and poetry and is important for its moral lessons as well as being a source of information and entertainment.

old would amuse herself? While Leon was living we never went to that house. He probably didn't allow Rebecca to go. After he died we would go two or three times a week, with me always as a cover. The unhappy widow paying social calls with her daughter. Rebecca never went to the cemetery because it depressed her. She said that Leon wasn't really in the tomb but in her heart. How ridiculous! Leon in Rebecca's heart in Carmela's house while the two of them whispered and laughed and made me leave if I tried to come in. They talked on the telephone very softly. Until that afternoon when Rebecca said she had a terrible headache and Carmela said she should lie down a while and then insisted that I go with her to the park. Like I was some five-year old or an imbecile. They would have given me candy if they'd had some. When we got to the park, Carmela sat down on a bench and said: Run around over there. As incredible as it seems, I sat down and asked God to send a downpour—a great, huge deluge that would soak her completely.It wouldn't matter that I got wet as well. I asked it with all of my heart, but God must be deaf. People walked through the park and went in and out of stores. Why couldn't I become one of those people who were walking all around me? A little girl fell down, scraped her knee, and cried. The mother came running to pick her up, carefully cleaned the knee, blew on the wound to dry it and then carried the little girl away. Was it that afternoon? Was I perhaps the one who fell? The park smelled wet but it never rained. The sun was an orange you could look up at. The air around me was suffocating and I couldn't take it any longer. Why didn't I run home without saying anything to Carmela? She would have looked for me for a while and then would have gone to tell Rebecca: "She got lost in the park." She might not even have been alarmed. I was so well brought up, so obedient: "Let's go look for mother, let's go, let's go." And she: "let's wait a while, would you like to look at the stores?" "I want to go, I want to look for my mother!" I can still remember the warm flush on her face. "Trouble-making, ill-bred little girl." A snake hissing the words. I didn't grab her by the hair and drag her through the park. I didn't rip her dress and leave her naked in front of everyone. And I was capable of walking along with her to the house, crossing the living room and the dining room to the patio, the hall to the room, the room empty, the bed empty, the bedspread and pillows on the bench in front of the dressing table and Rebecca's belt, watch and necklace on the dressing table itself, and Rebecca coming out of the bathroom combing her hair. What happened? Rebecca finishes combing her hair, applies makeup, and then puts on her watch, belt and necklace. And the whole time Carmela is opening and shutting her mouth, talking, getting worked up, becoming hoarse, and her sounds are swallowed up by the bed, empty, white, and sunken in the middle. Carmela's bed.

Luisa

Rebecca should not have done that to you. She was a widow and free
and she didn't need anyone to serve as a cover. I don't know why she
was so worried about what people would say when she had already
decided to leave the country. Of course the criticism would have been
harsh. The husband barely two months dead and she's already out
seeking consolation. People judge just by appearances, even you. I
don't know if I should tell you this or if I will help destroy the only
thing you love and respect, but I feel dirty hearing you talk that
way. I hope you can understand. When Leon died, it had been over
a year since he and Rebecca had sexual relations; they slept in the
bed like brother and sister. She was young and full of desire. She
never complained and I'm sure that if he had been living she would
never have gone near another man. I could tell you that the cause
of all of it was that he had had a heart attack and in one sense that
would be true, although not entirely true. You said that Rebecca had
been the lover and I the wife. Ever since I came to this house I began
to take charge of things and little by little Leon got accustomed to
discussing all the daily details with me. Rebecca didn't want to be
bothered with that sort of thing. One night, one of the many nights
when Leon got home late and found me awake he stroked my hair
and told me: "It took me a long time to learn how to see you, Luisa,
and now I can't offer you anything. I'm sorry." I answered him: I
have everything I want. And that was true. I loved him from the
very beginning, from those first days in which he took an interest in Rebecca and I was happy with his affection and kindnesses
without hoping for more. I suffered the day of the wedding, for the
first time seeing them kiss, realizing that he would not be mine,
and that I could not touch and embrace him like she could. When
they were on their honeymoon I suffered more. I understood that
my life would be worth nothing without seeing him, speaking with
him, or touching his hand or arm just casually. Rebecca made that
and much more possible. I shared everything with him except his
bed. After that late night conversation, he allowed himself to caress
me sometimes, always careful to not go too far. Then came the first
heart attack, which affected him some, but not totally. Rebecca cried
with me in the kitchen all morning. "He just can't any longer," she
told me, "he's not well." "Give him time," I advised. She looked at
me. "You understand him," she said, "help him." I felt confused and
embarrassed. "Ever since I came I've done nothing except try to help
both of you." She shook her head. "I know, but he needs you more
now." I didn't know how to take her words. I turned them around
and around in my head and the night we stayed together very late
watching a movie, when he began to caress my hair and kiss me on

the neck I decided that Rebecca had wanted to give me a great deal of leeway. I never dared to let her see; neither did he. We kept up appearances because we felt that it would be a big problem if she had to face it, but I've always believed she knew. That day in the cemetery when I told her that I preferred to stay in Cuba where my loved ones were buried, her response was: "They're more yours than mine." And when she called from Varadero, gone crazy, crying, and talking incoherently, until I managed to understand that you had escaped, she said: "I'm going, I can't make her come with me, she, too, has chosen you." It must have been very hard. And don't say that she asked for it. People don't always do what they should, or what they want to do, but they generally do what they are capable of doing. We're all somewhat egotistical and if we make sacrifices for someone it is almost always because we enjoy that sacrifice or because it pleases us or because the sacrifice is not that great. I probably should have said nothing. Who knows if with time you might have come to understand and forgive Rebecca without my needing to explain that there is plenty of blame for everyone. And, who knows if now you'll be able to pardon Leon and me.

Translation by Anne Fountain

The Lady with the Pooch

Jesús David Curbelo

A naked woman is a pretty common sight. But if she's leaning against a dog, a guy starts to take notice. Especially when it dawns on him, after he picks his jaw up off the floor, that the animal will play an important role in the drama that's about too unfold. And so it was: the fifth time I visited Astrid's home she received me in her birthday suit. After she spied me through the peep hole, she opened just the top half of the door and whispered, "Hurry. Get in here." I heard the latch click behind me, then came face to face with that marvel of a girl who, with a devilish look in her eye, was caressing her German shepherd's neck.

I met her at the writers' roundtable where I was jabbering away. She said to me, "You're Damaso, right? I'm Astrid."

"Nice to meet you," I murmured, as she held out her hand with long, purple nails.

Everything about her reminded me of a vampire's victim: tall, slim, dark circles under her eyes, mauve lipstick and a Modigliani neck ripe for sucking, biting, licking or any other lecherous verbs that came to mind. She was wearing shorts so short the threads hanging from their unraveling hem grazed the tops of her sculpted white thighs, against which stood out, like a tattoo, a thicket of ink-black locks that hung almost to her knees. A pink leotard covered her torso and thrust her large breasts forward; her sharply outlined nipples held me spellbound until she said:

"I'm a friend of Gabriel's. He's told me so much about you."

"Thanks, old buddy," I thought, reminded of how Gabriel sent to my office a pleiad of nymphs who fancied themselves poetesses, who shyly clutched their ubiquitous composition book—with a famous actor's picture on the cover—which contained the verses they thought were as good as Alejandra Pizarnik's. Their poems were almost always terrible and the authors were bonbons who melted into a pool of honey at the slightest innuendo. The story always ended the same way: they'd go to bed with me, for the moment spurning their boyfriends and lovers of their dreams, only to disappear later with lightning speed, disillusioned by my lack of enthusiasm for their talent.

"I write, too, y'know," Astrid continued with the next phase of the ritual I knew by heart.

"Well, if you like, I'll take a look at your work. Poems, right?" I asked, as I completed the third phase.

"Of course. Prose is a genre for older writers," Astrid answered, straying from the script.

"So, how old are you?" I queried offhandedly, trying to get back on track.

"Nineteen. Same as Rimbaud when he started to write." She strayed from the role of the sweet young thing with long hair, wearing the ubiquitous thick-soled tennis shoes.

"You've read Rimbaud, Astrid?" I quizzed her, having no choice but to improvise.

"No, but Gabriel talks about him all the time. He says Rimbaud and Whitman invented twentieth-century poetry."

"Sure, in a way," I parried vaguely. Trying to get back on track, I added, "Well, so where're those poems of yours?" My curiosity always gets the better of me.

"Right here." She held out a stack of pages that were typed and paper-clipped in the upper left hand corner. "Don't go easy on me. I'm prepared for the worst."

I was devising ways to get her into bed, to put her in this or that position, do this and that move (that dazzled the girls every time), but in the blink of an eye she said, *"Ciao,"* and turned her back so quickly that it stopped me cold. I almost didn't get to ask:

"Astrid, how can I see you again . . . to tell you my opinion?"

"Oh, sorry. Here my address. But call before you come by, OK?"

And she was gone, leaving her calling card in my hand.

To my surprise, Astrid's poems were the best I'd read by a novice. Still, it was clear she didn't know one iota about literature. That I had to correct. I had to give her a form that would bring her throbbing naiveté to the forefront and bring out the passion lying deep beneath her surface, like a mysterious current. I re-read her original poems, afraid I was getting carried away not by their literary merits but by the author's quivering tits—tits that cried out for the master's touch from under her leotard. The poems withstood the test. They talked about love, as usual, but a love carved deep by larceny, a love whose wounds revealed to the world death, lies, loneliness, anguish, uncertainty and all the things (God love 'em) that impinge upon a poet's repose.

A week later I dialed Astrid's number. As soon as she said, "Come on over," I flew to the door of her two-story cottage that had a garden, fence, garage and glass Venetian blinds. At the door awaited the sweet poet inquiring in English:

"Well then . . ."

"Well your poems are . . ." I replied in English. Then in Spanish, I enumerated the virtues and defects I'd seen and the easiest way they could be retooled.

"Perfect! Just what I need to get my book off the ground. Your advice is really terrific. Did you mark the poems or do I need to memorize what you're saying?"

I told her I'd made some marks, but if she liked we—the plural gave away my willingness to be transformed, unconditionally, into her assistant—could take her poems in hand until they were ready for publication.

She jumped at that. "You think they could be published? Where? Is there anything you can do?"

I said yes, convinced that *yes* was the *open sesame* to Astrid's legs. I put out of my mind the fact that I was sweating ink to get my own book into print, sending it to any prize that came along, and then enduring the sinking feeling of waiting for a verdict, which was unfavorable most of the time, even when it wasn't shamelessly fixed to benefit someone's protégé.

We spent the afternoon sitting on the porch, crossing out a line here, searching for the exact idea there, just the right adjective, the superfluous word. It dawned on me that, for the first time, I was sinking my claws into someone else's poem, molding it as if it were my own. To be truthful, I hate the literary teaching profession. The way I see it, writing is a field where a person should learn what's possible in a fierce battle between language and plot. No one should to tell you that removing and adding commas and nouns will earn you the right to posterity. Yet, Astrid's body was in the mix now, the female mammalian smell that emanated from her armpits, from between her legs, from the air she moved through, leaving behind a desirable perfume that easily conquered a rake like me, and that was beforethe inescapable force of that pair of tits.

On my second visit she introduced me to her father: a laid-back guy in his forties, dressed to the nines. He didn't seem to mind that daughter's new friendship was with a guy ten years her senior who he could plainly see was wooing her. Her mother, she explained, lived at the beach, where she'd worked in tourism for a decade. She had divorced Astrid's dad because she'd had the hots for some teenager. She'd replaced him with a string of other guys, so many that Astrid didn't know who was the love of her mom's life at the moment. They were cordial, nothing more. Despite her mother's open-mindedness, Astrid detected in her mother's behavior a certain decadence she didn't want to lower herself to . . . At this point she became exasperated. She didn't like to ask for anyone's help. What's more she didn't want me to push her into a particular focus for her book. Her tirade was followed by my apology and a conciliatory torrent of words about how, in the end, the essence of the poems comes from your head and heart. I'm just a skilled craftsman who can fine-tune your talent at this unavoidable stage of apprenticeship. Astrid smiled, flattered by my little speech and burst into a flood of reasons to justify our continuing.

On the third visit, I (we) came up with the title for her book. We'd give it an English title—*Alice Has Gone*. The title was the same as one of the poems in which Astrid confessed how she had cast off infancy and lost her virginity and her spirit in two or three run-ins she'd had with the wolf pack that was our world, where everyone wanted to gobble her up by appealing to faith, reason, justice or love. That day, she declared to me her need to get down to business, step into the spotlight not as a lovely libertine but as a role model for everyone else. Her father always tried to get her involved in something useful, she said. He pushed her into studying languages (English, French, Italian), shorthand, typing, computers, any other field that would help her deal with modern life.

"But being someone's secretary is not my life's dream. I want to have my own secretary."

Although she sounded overly ambitious, I thought it didn't hurt to have the illusion of transforming herself into an efficient executive with a big paycheck, her own house, car and a bullet-proof intimacy. Still, I argued, a Hollywood dream is hard to achieve. There's always that person who spends her whole life pursuing status, only to realize in the end that this was not her true path, that she had cast aside a much more clear-cut path when there was still time.

"Cheap philosophy," she snapped. "You have to be the best at what you do. That's the only way to get where you want to go."

And at that point, I saw that Astrid was also determined to be a winner, one of those people who don't back down, but who leap the imaginary bar of fulfillment a couple of inches higher than her sisters. Instead of scaring me off, that discovery turned me into a very nice, very adolescent guy. The only thing that occurred to me to do was smile and succumb to the spiderweb that was enfolding me.

I didn't see her for several months. She disappeared the way she arrived: unceremoniously. I didn't even get a good-bye note. How was it possible that I could miss her so much after such a short time? I'd gotten so used to having her around. I thought about her non-stop: Astrid at breakfast, midmorning on a boring day at work, during lunch gulped down on the run, in the afternoons as I corrected the manuscript of some erotic novel. My fantasies killed any desire I might have had to be satisfied in my ramshackle marriage, so I took refuge at night in front of the TV. It protected my wife and me from conversations that invariably ended in a fight. The trick of masturbating in the bath like some pimply-faced kid wasn't enough to exorcise my bad mood. Over and over I constructed and deconstructed situations where we would reach an agreement, we'd kiss and have sex for hours in the weirdest places. Then we'd start all over again. I'd analyze our dates, searching for the moment when I should have said what I didn't or couldn't have known to say. Now I was trying to fix that moment in a vicious cycle that left me exhausted and spent. "Maybe she didn't like me. Maybe she just used me to put her book together and she figured out she had to flirt with me. Maybe she knows I'm a sucker for her type." I tortured myself with fruitless comparisons to the sexy stars she'd mentioned in passing—Kevin Costner, Rob Lowe, Brad Pitt or that Mexican soap opera star, Cesar Evora. I kept getting tangled up in brain-teasers and tongue-twisters that shattered my track record as a professional seducer.

"Hey, Damaso. Long time no see." I snapped out of my daydream, aware that someone was calling me from the other side of the street. When I turned around: Astrid.

"Hi," was all I managed.

"I need you," she said as she kissed me on the cheek. And she added, "There's a prize that's perfect for my book. Could you help me with a re-write?"

"Sure," I answered, forgetting all about my plans to get revenge, to put distance between us when she turned up, to show her I wasn't the kind of guy you can use. I said I'd check my calendar because I was loaded down with work. She said it's not much, just a minor revision. Of course, I didn't hesitate for a second: when should we meet—not letting her get a word in edgewise—how about tonight? She said, looking down, doubtful, her house was out, they're having a party. I said I'll pick you up, let's go somewhere. Then I added, inspired, how about a restaurant? She said great and mentioned an expensive seafood place. Then, half repentant, I put on my *ay mi madre* face and made the excuse that it's hard to get a reservation. Astrid came back with don't worry, thank God Dad has a friend there, *Oh* and I'll pay, I know it's really expensive.

I started to protest politely but got nowhere. The next thing I knew, I was hanging around the door of that place, waiting for her in the half light. The book was just a pretext. I knocked back a couple of drinks and she explained that she'd spent the tourist season with her mother. We started to chat. Then we careened off course into the emotional realm when I recklessly proposed a flexible, unconventional relationship based on passion, not affection.

"Hey!" she laughed. "That wasn't so hard, was it? I thought you were shy. Not you! *Bam!* You say it all in one breath, then sit there waiting for my answer."

"Almost all," I countered, with a lack of tact I cynically call sincerity. "I'm married."

"I know, I don't care. I'm gonna be with you, not her."

With that, she sealed the pact, but the traditional kiss didn't materialize until much, much later, when I hinted, "We can go to a place I know of close by. My hideaway. It's quiet and discrete."

"Sounds good," she murmured. Off we went to Abel's mother's apartment. His mother, who was in no hurry to return from the States, had bequeathed that hideaway to her son and me for our extramarital shenanigans. Astrid played the role of the good girl who dwells in a romance novel but who lets herself be swept away in the whirlwind of my lasciviousness. As we caressed each other with lips, tongues, teeth, hands, thighs, and arms, she stripped, while making it seem like I'd undressed her. In my initial ecstasy, provoked by the abundant foliage of her pubic down, I spread her across the bed face up and ran my mouth over her entire geography, delighting in valleys and crevices, hills and lagoons with the skill of a surveyor taking great pains not to miss an inch of ground. When my tongue had circumvented her armpits, butt, and inside her thighs and was poised to penetrate her savagely, ready to deposit the power of my language and the fertility of my saliva, Astrid lightly grasped me by the hair and panted, "No, please, I don't like that." Although her rejection inhibited me for a moment, I opted to slide on top of her and bury my sex in a humidity that eagerly swallowed it all, wrung it, rubbed it, squeezed it and made it eject its sap amid a gyration of sighs, words, sweat, sodomizing fingers, bites and rasping breaths of pleasure.

Astrid granted me a half truce during which she described traumas, cited a list of the men she'd been with and confessed that no other human had ever given her such pleasure the first time. That triggered her attack on me at all four points of the compass in a rare blend of candor and debasement. My blood heated to the temperature of her crater, where I hurled myself again and again until, just barely conscious, I saw it was time to quit being joined like Siamese twins, shower, get dressed, take my captive home, promising to come by the next morning, and make it home before my wife finished her shift at the hospital.

Ever since I was little, I've been afraid of dogs. All dogs. Even the ones barking behind a window. Or the ones that would make mincemeat of you on the street if they weren't under their master's control. That's why I froze, in the middle of Astrid's living room, when she urged me to pet that monster named Herod.

"Thanks, but he's not my type. I prefer you naked."

"Well, get used to him. Herod's my protector at times like these."

"When the villain tries to get you into the sack?"

"No. When my dad and step mom take the kids to the beach for a week and leave me all alone so I can invite the villain over and prove Herod's an angel." She savored each letter with the pleasure that only someone who offers and reclaims Paradise can.

Without further ado, she sat astride the animal's head and rubbed her crotch against his snout. Then she sprawled out on the couch and let that creature's tongue go in search of her scent, familiar after God knows how many scenes like that. Astrid stroked his ribs with a growing frenzy, while her right foot slid down his belly till it perched on the red appendix of his sex. Despite my disgust I had an unstoppable erection. Astrid grabbed my waist with her right hand, drew me to her and took my member in the blink of an eye. I became one of the legs in that unholy triangle in which the dog launched his sperm to the ceiling and mine went into Astrid's mouth. She seemed to levitate amid Herod's licks, my pelvic thrusts and her own hands, which were stimulating her nipples and ass.

"Now that's sucking! Everything else is just talk," Astrid pronounced, lying limp. Not wasting any time, she led us (the dog and me) up the stairs to the bedroom, urging me to strip along the way. There, as if by accident, a gigantic bed was placed in front of an even more gigantic mirror that reflected our images contorting in the preamble to sexual frenzy. Astrid climbed on top of me and busied herself with spreading the fluids of her vagina over every nook and cranny of me. Then she begged, "Take me from behind, *papi*." Trying to contribute even a tiny kernel of my imagination, I picked up a deodorant bottle off her dressing table and stuck it into her vulva, while I pried open her tight anal sphincter with spit and perseverance. At that moment Herod, doubtless drawn by the girl's aroma, greedily licked my back, butt, balls, and finally even my ass, giving me a huge charge that accelerated my movements inside Astrid. Possessed from the front with the improvised dildo and from the rear by my phallus, she lost control of her undulations and a preconscious mechanism took over, purely and physically instinctive, born of the pristine nucleus from which spring pleasure and agony, thirst and hurricanes, fever and the oasis of spying ourselves again in the mirror: two sinners and a beast roasting in ecstasy in some dark caldron in Hell.

That morning we leapt the barrier and set off to try out infinite combinations (the dog here, there, in this, in that, with this in his paw and that in our mouth), baptize objects (perfume bottles, douche bag, cucumbers, bananas, bottle necks), and we became the founders of a cabal. Our need sharpened, and we came up with bolder and bolder variations until, on the eve of her family's return, Astrid posed a panic-stricken question:

"What'll we do afterwards?"

"I don't know. I guess we'll keep on like this," I answered, not understanding the question.

"I'm talking about a different *afterwards*. What we have'll end one fine day. Where'm I gonna find a guy as crazy as you, who'll share me with Herod?"

From that day on, the lady with the pooch became a drug. I found any excuse to be away from home to chase after them and fornicate with them: in her father's cottage, Abel's apartment or dimly lit alleys where we fearlessly took chances, protected by the ferocious-looking German shepherd.

My home life became even more vapid. Over and over, I shrunk from contact with my wife in favor of my exotic fantasies. No matter how much she improvised to give me pleasure, she couldn't come anywhere close to the multitude of sensations, whims, and dark appetites the dog and the girl aroused. That finally did in my marriage. The angry looks, shouts, vile word, and insults we traded became common knowledge in the neighborhood along with the jarring clatter of broken plates, the crash of pots and pans against the wall and even a few reciprocated slaps. One day I left that hell hole for good after I broke the tape player to smithereens, insulted my wife in a way I could never take back and finally hit her square in the face with a fresh tortilla that went flying out of the frying pan despite my effort to control myself.

The situation was no better at my mother's house. Mom had the terrible habit of treating me like a baby at the tit. *Where're you going? Who're you going out with? When're you coming back?* were her favorite questions. On top of that, she constantly quizzed me about the state of my finances. She figured out that I had no cash, and pulled money out of the air to smooth over my bad temper when she got too overprotective. Even so, my diabolical side always won out, and I opted to fight back against maternal love by drinking so much it freed me from her sermons. I countered her accusations of abuse and insolence with such furor and violence that I got my point across. To top it off, the rum was flowing freely. Astrid's father supported his family by making and selling a bootleg whiskey popularly known as "train spark." He fermented molasses from the sugar mills in water, and then boiled it in enormous pressure cookers. The vapor flowed out of the cooker through valves, wound along serpentine paths, and was cooled under the tank's spout, then finally filtered drop by drop, through a funnel containing activated charcoal and other chemical devices. The result was a hellacious alcohol that shredded your liver and left the taste of guilt and misery in your mouth and on your soul.

We went through Astrid's poetry manuscript so many times we nearly set a record. We typed it up and she went in person to turn it in at the contest headquarters. The prize consisted of three hundred pesos and publication. The bloom of skepticism was on her face, but when all was said and done, I knew she had faith in my expertise and secretly aspired to make off with the reward. Then it happened: I was invited to be a judge. I turned it down. The envoy insisted. He pointed out my professional success, my reputation for being incorruptible and the need to choose each judge carefully, so the verdict wouldn't be in doubt and wouldn't affect the prestige of the sponsoring institution. I accepted reluctantly, not wanting to offend such an effusive admirer and the organization he represented. Astrid jumped for joy when she found out. After mulling it over, she said:

"You'll know what to do. No matter what happens, I trust you."

The following week I received the package of twenty-three manuscripts. After the first reading, I eliminated thirteen whose authors didn't have a clue about what poetry was. After the next reading only six survived, including Astrid's. The other five remaining contestants fell into two categories: two were friends and three I didn't know. With so much on the line, I felt out the second of the trio of judges (I couldn't count on the third judge since severe aesthetic differences separated us and had turned him into my enemy). He said what I wanted to hear. He proposed nearly the same finalists. "The book by the girl is very picturesque but it lacks something," he pronounced. My risky second attempt—sweetened by two bottles of liquor—drifted into a long discussion that contributed beyond measure to finding the missing "something." I praised *Alice Has Gone* to high heavens. It was easy. In a way, I was merely speaking well of myself. Three days later we got together with the remaining judge and my new-found comrade-in-arms crushed him with solid arguments (I intervened only when necessary). The ruling was unanimous in favor of Astrid's poetry collection.

At the award ceremony, my friends left the hall without saying good-bye. Gabriel glared at me and made a gesture that meant "this time you've gone too far." My fellow judges frowned in disgust when they saw how I had manipulated the judging to give the award to my lover. My reputation and the respect people had for me went to hell. Now I was just one more of those immoral people like all the rest. But I didn't care. In the crowd, struggling to keep a grip on Herod's leash, Astrid smiled, promising me glory.

"I'm leaving, Damaso. I can't stand this city or the people a minute longer." Astrid declared, two weeks later, during a late breakfast at Abel's mother's house.

"What? Where're you going?" I inquired a bit harshly.

"You think you control me?" She looked at me mockingly. "I guess I can go wherever I want, whenever I want."

"What I meant was, why are you leaving now," I replied, as I

tried to calm down and study her, "when things are going so well
between us?"

"Going so well?" she grumbled. "Your teeny weenie salary as a literary editor barely covers your smokes. Your wife no longer supports
you, so you can't write, and your mother's getting tired of taking care
of you. As for me, I don't work and I can't support you. Daddy, who
always sees the big picture, has started to ask questions . . ."

"OK, but . . ." I stammered, completely stymied.

"*But* nothing. We can't go on like this. We're both adults. You know
what they say, 'where there's money, there's freedom.' If Daddy and
your mom pay for everything, they'd make our life hell with all their
conditions. I can't handle that. Mom got me a job as a tour guide
have an interview tomorrow with the head of the agency."

"Astrid!"

"*Astrid* what? Someone's got to hustle up some cash, right? Doesn't
look like it's gonna be you. On top of that, you're not writing a fucking line."

"I thought that . . ."

"That you were gonna live on credit? No, *papi.* You need to be
someone's boy toy. My boy toy, that is. This little shit-eating girl
is gonna get down to business and see if she can save some money.
Maybe you'll want to marry her . . ." she paused to gauge the effect
of her tirade and, a bit let down, continued. "You need to get your
act together, stop chasing after culture and go into tourism, like
me. With the languages you know and your looks, Mom could find
something for you in no time. Housing wouldn't be a problem. After
all the nice things I've said about you, she thinks you're a good
guy."

Without knowing it, Astrid had dashed our relationship. That
argument was the same one I endured from my wife. Always the
same opinions, the same answers, the same quarrels. True, breaking
up was not a good plan, but not as bad as battling stupid tourists who
thought I was some servile native willing to put up with any humiliation just to acquire a portion of the meager sum they had scraped
together after months of sacrifice for their giddy Caribbean spree. I
said flat-out, "*No*, let's find a third option," and offered several plans,
trying in vain to come up with a solution.

"I'm sorry, Damaso. My mind's made up." Seeing me turn away
at that, she softened a bit. "This isn't the end of the world. I'll come
see you on the weekends. Or you can come to Mom's place. She won't
mind if we stay there a couple of nights."

Off she went. In a few days she called me at work but I wasn't
there. In her message she said they'd hired her on the spot and left
a number where I could get in touch with her. She reminded me

to come see her that weekend. I didn't leave the office for the next three afternoons, a slave to the phone, lifting up the receiver with the childish hope of hearing Astrid's voice telling me that it was a disaster and that she'd be back in the city any time now. Friday morning I made up my mind. I wouldn't go to the beach. I had to show that chick I wasn't a sap ready to jump at her every whim. Surely first thing on Monday Astrid would call, asking for forgiveness or at least demanding an explanation.

That didn't happen. She never called again. I never could get in touch with her at the number she left. "Who's calling?" asked a receptionist's voice. I got one story after another, about how she's on the yacht with some Italians, in the hotel with some Canadians, or playing badminton with some newly arrived Germans. I had no luck contacting her through her father. He suggested I talk to his ex-wife. Maybe I could get a line on Astrid's whereabouts from her. Nothing. Her mother never answered my SOS. I sent two or three feverish letters that went unanswered. I went crazy. My alcohol consumption and absences from work doubled. Without Astrid the world was shit.

Then the roof caved in: my wife filed for a divorce, I got fired, Abel and Gabriel refused to listen to my laments and told me how stupid I'd been, my mother cut back on my financial aid and I discovered that Astrid had taken Herod with her. So I made a plan: with what little money I had left, I bought a German shepherd puppy and tried to train him in fellatio and licking. No use. My phobic terror of dogs got in the way of any interaction with the animal. I tried in vain to persuade the most depraved of my ex-lovers: those who could wouldn't and those who would were busy. I also dared to propose the experiment to the many faceless girls I went to bed with to console myself. Chaos. Soon after I'd sold the dog for half what he cost me and redoubled my efforts to drink myself to death, Astrid's only letter arrived.

Dear Damaso:

Life is unsettlingly complex. And one must take advantage of one's opportunities. As you can see, I'm writing from Düsseldorf. I've been living here for a month. When you kept me waiting for so long, it was hard to forgive you and even harder to get a grip on my affection for you. Then I met Jorgen. He's a rich industrialist's son and he fell madly and sincerely in love with me. Just like in *Pretty Woman*, you must be thinking. That's one way to look at it. Rest assured, he was the only one and I didn't beg him to take me to Europe. Since we met, he has proposed to me. His parents, who came to Cuba for a vacation, love me. At first I considered turning him down, but I realized that one doesn't get too many chances in life. One must seize them before it's too late.

You said that yourself, right? So I accepted Jorgen as my husband and overnight became a young society lady. Prostitute? You could say that, although to my way of thinking, a very high class one. Perhaps we women were put on this earth to find a husband who'll support us and plant the seed of strong, outstanding offspring. I believe that's the reason for adultery, prostitution and many of the wars past and future: the search for balance between love and happiness. In a way, I love Jorgen and I'm happy with him. I'm gong to try to return the huge favor he did me when he ushered me into his world. You were very important to me, but in the end you were unattainable. We weren't gong anywhere. You don't inspire confidence for two reasons: you love yourself too much and you can't guarantee your own well-being. That's not a put down, just a eulogy. Protect your freedom from other women who, like me, will pass through your life and will be dazzled.

Kisses, good luck and don't waste your talent.

PS I forgot to ask three things of you: understand me, take care of *Alice Has Gone* and look after Herod, my other great loss. He loves you (in his own way, of course).

Astrid

Inside the envelope was a picture of her in winter clothes with a blond guy, handsome as Prince Charming, and a black Doberman with excellent markings. On the back it said:

Jorgen couldn't resist my admiration for dogs so he gave me this one. His name is Pilate. How's that for coming full circle?

It took a long time to recover from the alcoholic crisis I'd slipped into. I rejected all company except for the bottle and, at first, Herod, whom I'd collected from Astrid's mother's house like the spoils of a lost war. But it didn't work. Without the girl's scent, the animal was incapable of giving pleasure. Instead he would growl, offended at my tentative attempts to go near him. We felt the same distress, lovers abandoned by the bitch in heat who has quit wagging her tail in front of our muzzle, wafting the aroma of her sex. Two males cut to shreds by the absence of the same female couldn't live together. I swapped Herod for six bottles of vodka. I submerged the zoophilous chapter of my life in the amnesia of a drunken binge that lasted nearly a year, if you add up all the drinks I imbibed, the scenes I caused, the hangovers, the vague and traumatic sexual episodes with women each more despicable than the one before, the fears, the blaming, the police stations, the loss of jobs and getting drunk all over again to erase the mishaps that were multiplying. Then someone handed me a lovely copy of *Alice Has Gone*.

Astrid decided, who knows when, to dedicate her book to me. The dedication read "To Damaso, his book," Of course it was. Why didn't I see that from the start? I was the writer. Astrid Torres Peralta was only a pseudonym for the female side that was returning to me after flirting with a handful of promiscuous readers. That saved me. I figured it was my duty to burnish my sullied soul by writing a torrent of poems that would restore my image—in my eyes and in everyone else's. I wasn't going to let myself be done in by an apocryphal spirit, by someone who existed just to inspire me to write that poem. She'd played the part of an innocent lamb eager to hook up with the hungry wolf, who didn't hesitate to tattoo her innocence with a series of degradations. Sure I'd made her swoon, but she abandoned me in a blink of an eye, refusing to be trapped in any prison except one of her own making.

Through fiction, I conjured up the truth of such a ridiculous time and prepared for the moment—not long in coming—when I started to write *Alice Comes Back*. In it I'd see Astrid get out of a tourist Jeep, walk over, greet me with a barely perceptible wink and not even have the decency to ask about Herod. Really it wouldn't be necessary. The lamb of my vision would be leading her new toy, the dog Pilate, by the leash; with the other hand, a devilish look in her eye, she'd be caressing the arm of her latest shepherd, the German.

Translation by Pamela Carmell

How Much I Love You

Jesús David Curbelo

For Tula, her story

Marcial Méndez was obsessed with two things: women and synonyms. When it came to women, things always went badly for him. Synonyms cost him friendships, jobs and all kinds of opportunities in life. In a conversation, he'd quit listening to what people were saying and get waylaid by some colorful word and by hunting for equivalents. At that moment nothing else on the face of this earth mattered. One synonym called up another, then another, until Marcial's head was spinning with so many words. Finally the people he was talking to threw up their hands. That happened with women, too. Once their initial enchantment with his striking good looks and his flowery, gushing eloquence had worn off, they were turned off by his distraction or his mania to stitch together concepts, phrases, and paragraphs all centered on a particular idea.

In those days, only Lucía had endured his verbal onslaught. Now here he was on this balmy afternoon, a perfect chance to reflect as he adjusted his step to the pace of his thoughts, tightening his grip on the metal strap, looking at the ground, sighing, going over and over those days. He'd forgotten that some palm reader, soothsayer, witch, sorceress, fortune teller, oracle or daughter of an African witch doctor had predicted a horrible, lunatic end to his love for Lucía.

He met her, such an enchantress, temptress, in the hustle and bustle of people lined up in front of the movie theatre. Her slender, delicate figure caught his eye as she touched her body, pretending to hunt for something that bothered her. She's careful and discrete, he thought, embarrassed to scratch in public, so her hands steal over arms as if stroking velvet. But he'd been watching her for a while and knew for sure she was scratching, rubbing, poking, chafing, scraping away at her skin.

He sidled up to her and whispered in her ear something banal to get the ball rolling. Something is really bugging you. Mosquitoes, I guess, she conceded. He blamed such an unbearable riot of mosquitoes on the rain, the puddles, the trees in the park nearby and the tangle of bushes in need of pruning, along with local health conditions and the shortage of pesticides. She agreed with him. He paid for their tickets and took her lightly by the elbow, certain his luck was changing.

It was. They were born to see that movie together where the leading man is chased through the jungle and has to survive swamps, wild animals, raging rivers, cannibals and a string of other dangers to marry the heroine and return to his ranch and live happily ever after. Marcial felt her twist and turn nervously in her seat. It must be the suspense, he told himself, but after a while all her moving around, her restlessness, her agitation grew worse and he started to lose his cool.

Something wrong? he asked. She blamed the mosquitoes again despite the air conditioning and he, bold and audacious, didn't wait for a better sign. He got all cutesy, reciting that ditty his schoolmates made him read in their gross-out autograph session so long ago. Before he could get to the last verse, the audience yelled for him to shut up and he was forced to swallow his words which got all balled up in his throat: Iwouldliketobeamosquitoandgetinsideyourmosquitonetandtellyouinalowvoicehowmuchiloveyou.

She got the idea and laughed, amused. He rubbed his hands together. He'd scored, closed the deal, sealed the pact; he could kiss those lonely Saturday nights good-bye. No more hanging around watching girls or being the third wheel with friends who dragged him along to bars and stadiums. Lucía was still restless and Marcial Méndez suggested, irresistibly, "Let's take a walk when we get out of here. We could get a drink, talk for a while, maybe get some dinner."

She agreed, and Marcial, ready to shoulder the expense, also shouldered her little bugs. The mosquito in the movie became an ant in the bar, a fly in the street and a butterfly in the restaurant. She allowed him to walk her home—he only had to ask once—where it was more of the same, mixed with hope. A beetle, a cricket, a spider, a fly, a lightning bug, or some other kind of insect, predator or vermin that drove her to shrug, gnaw on herself, dig into every square inch of her body. When she couldn't stand it any longer, she excused herself, went to the restroom, turned her clothes and underwear inside out, then returned, all smiles saying it was just my imagination. Then she realized it was nearly her bedtime and Marcial Méndez hadn't managed to get more than a few measly kisses.

He looked at her legs, thighs, hips, eyes, lips and convinced himself that the heavenly girl Mann had imagined couldn't have been shaped any other way. Lucía was a princess. There was even a pea under her mattress. He figured that out in no time at that crummy hotel they'd checked into, seeking privacy. Give it a rest, Lucía, protested Marcial Méndez in the middle of a fit of scratch me here and check me out there. You're too old for Hans Christian Andersen fairy tales. Then moved to tears by all that scratching, she defended herself, saying I warned you, Marcial. I can't sleep or relax or even concentrate anywhere but in my own bed. He took that to be a good sign as he was leaving in the morning without having made love, dead tired from the fruitless search for fleas, bedbugs, lice and chiggers.

Every weekend it was the same absurd, tragic, hellish scene until he saw no alternative: Marcial Méndez got married and settled into Lucía's room, her bed, her sheets, her pillow: An extremely tidy oasis where she was isolated from invasions of arthropods and coleopterans. But he harbored doubts. Could this have been a stratagem, a plan, a ruse, a dirty trick to lure an unwary man into the ordeal of matrimony? Looking into Lucía's sweet suffering face and seeing the unceasing fury of her hands searching all over her body for the lone bug that got away, Marcial was persuaded that there was no deception. He took pride in her nakedness and her immodesty, and in the fact that they could alleviate the fatiguing search each time they reached the pinnacle of love making.

Admittedly, between his job, visits to in-laws and parents, and a couple of flings on the side that the very handsome Marcial Méndez allowed himself out of spite or out of the pleasure of being even more frustrated, his time at Lucía's side was limited to taking her to bed and molding their flesh in the act of surrendering, offering, relinquishing themselves to a whirlwind that exorcised her itching and left her in a state of grace until dawn. Most of the time. One night Marcial awoke with a start to feel Lucía's legs locked around his, twitching uncontrollably. A rictus of pain slashed across her face. Fearing a bad dream, Marcial brought her back to her senses. But it was worse. Check here, in my groin, I think there's a bug in there doing cartwheels. Crabs. He was horrified, remembering his latest deceptions, frauds, adulteries, about how some unscrupulous beauty must have infected him with filthy, sucking lice that had turned up in his wife's crotch. He dreaded a fight that would take him back to those lonely Saturday nights, something he couldn't tolerate.

There's nothing wrong with you, nothing, he shouted, hysterical, trying to reassure himself that no critter was prowling around Lucía's pubic down. But she was in serious anguish. Know what? she confided. Lately I feel things crawling all over my skin. It's always been like that, he argued, as long as I've known you. I'll bet you're allergic. No, no, she broke in. This time it's different, it feels like they're inside me, floating around in my blood. In the next several days, he was afraid, ready to bolt, but he concealed it, joked around, pampered her, gave advice, kisses, and caresses. Asleep in his arms, Lucía was once again the heavenly girl, the princess from a distant land plagued by the pea. He kept recalling she'd been the girl of his dreams, the one he fell in love with. For her he was ready to take the biggest step of all, do the moral thing and create a family, something that usually did in other couples. He went even farther: he controlled his mania to eye the chicks, to propose weird rendezvous in some dark place, an elevator, a bus, a train or packed theater. Out in public he investigated her pelvic triangle, her buttocks, the small of her back, the swell of her breasts, as if finding his way back to Paradise depended on it. For her he even renounced synonyms and aspired to dumb down his language to a very basic level of communication, so she'd be happy and not overwhelmed in her affliction.

Still he worried when he saw her suffering and suggested that it might be bad circulation. That gave her hope, so they went to the doctor and inquired about the most effective cure. That wasn't it. They ruled out scabies, psoriasis, pitinasis and skin cancer; her blood sugar, platelets, her hemoglobin and the entire lymphatic system were normal; no parasite roamed around in her belly. Psychiatric tests yielded nothing out of the ordinary. But what had been uneasiness changed to desperation, frenzy and was never under control again. At all hours, night or day, he found her crazily raking her skin section by section, with a chilling, vehement, insane desire. He stopped having guests over, taking walks, going to social gatherings, because his private Lucía was revealing without shame all aspects of her mania. She talked about pruritis, rashes, bites, chafing and tingling and nothing else, at all hours of the day and night. Marcial Méndez feared her wild eyes, her unstoppable hands, her howls of fear and the negative side effects of taking the sedatives, drugs and potions they prescribed for her to drink, smear on, smell, put under the bed, around the patio or behind the door. He confessed to himself that he was powerless to live alongside this monster. He overcame the thought of being judged too self-centered, too cowardly and weak to confront life's difficulties and got up the courage to speak his mind. But he never had to go through with it. Wise nature played her part: Lucía died one morning in the middle of a microorganism attack. With hardly a fuss, her heart stopped beating. Too much excitement, the surprised doctor diagnosed. Marcial Méndez, a victim of mixed feelings, half sorrow, half stupor, sighed with relief.

Now, here he was on this balmy afternoon, a perfect chance to reflect. He adjusted his pace to the train of his thoughts, tightening his grip on the metal strap around the hearse. He sighed again, wondering whether, now that Lucía's lovely body was underground, she would have to endure the impertinence of earth worms, tape worms, cockroaches, mice and bacteria, whether such darkness would be enough to keep them from plaguing her forever. Without realizing, he let go of the galvanized ring on the side of the hearse and tried to wipe away the prickling feeling descending his forehead. There was nothing there, not even sweat. He looked up and saw that the chauffeur was driving with one hand, engrossed in a battle with some invisible presence in his hair. The mourner on his left was unbuttoning his shirt to dig immodestly in his armpits. The guy on the other side did the same. And then another guy. Then a woman. He looked back to the end of the line, refusing to believe what he saw: hundreds of faces with the same dazed look, brushing off their mourning coats, hats, skirts, ears, glasses, teeth. A strange laugh came to his lips. He stifled it in light of the solemn ceremony, although he had to admit how funny that pathetic coincidence was. It was the nightmare that completed his destiny. He tried to banish it from his thoughts along with the compelling desire to rub, scrape, scratch, brush himself off—and the urge to laugh. He couldn't help thinking that those bugs would get inside him and writhe around, frolic around, all the way up to his eyes. He let a belly laugh slip out, felt it change to tears, flights of fantasy, itches. And he let it all wash over him.

Translation by Pamela Carmell

Book Reviews

Jacques Jouet. *L'Amour comme on l'apprend à l'École hôtelière* [Love as one learns it at hotel school]. Paris: POL, 2006. 442pp. €22.90.

Since the early 1990s, Jacques Jouet has been hard at work on a vast, loosely-organized prose cycle entitled "La République roman" ("the republic of the novel" or "the novel of the republic"). That series now includes a score of works, the most recent of which is *L'Amour comme on l'apprend à l'École hôtelière*. Patently Balzacian in its conception (though it does not pretend to rival the Census Bureau), Jouet's project offers a wide-angle view of contemporary French society. Focusing in turn on the general and the local, on broad questions of social organization and on the fine grist of ordinary lives, Jouet has provided his readers with a constantly-ramifying account of lived experience, both collective and individual. Not coincidentally, he has also provided us with an intriguing set of case studies devoted to the potential of prose fiction today.

Jouet's latest novel traces the fortunes of a family, from the birth of Georges Romillat in 1930 to the death of his son, Sylvain, in 1987. The former signs on as Professor of Love at a Parisian hotel school—though his experience is very limited indeed, both in the art of love and in the craft of hotel management. He will prove to be an able learner, however, wooing and winning one of his former students, and buying a hotel in the far suburbs of Paris. Sylvain, the first of four children (he is followed by triplets, one of whom, Jiji, serves as Jacques Jouet's narrative voice), is as extraordinary a person as his father is ordinary. Together, in counterpoint, they play out the tensions between those two categories of experience. Jouet also constructs interesting tensions between the political and the personal, as the main events of contemporary French history—World War II, the Algerian War of Independence, May 1968—collide with the far more intimate events of quotidian family life in a dynamic of mutual interrogation. In an epilogue, Jouet speculates on how his own family history finds its way into this novel through permutation, displacement, and a deliberate refusal to supplement memory with prosthetics such as archival research or personal interviews. In those instances where his memory fails him, he tells us, he invents. One would expect nothing else from a novelist, of course, and it is precisely in its inventive character that this novel shines so brightly. [Warren Motte]

Azhar Abidi. *Passarola Rising*. Viking, 2006. 244pp. $21.95.

This brilliant novel is written for those of us who want to see new worlds, new boundaries (if they exist). It is a 'science fiction,' a thrilling meditation on the meaning of exile, exploration, and travel. We encounter two figures, Bartolemew, the builder of an 'airship,' the *Passarola*, and his younger brother, Alexandre. The book is narrated by Alexandre. He describes their adventures sixty years after the 'rising' of the *Passarola*; he is on land, a husband, an old man who maintains: "It is too late *now*. Old age is not *unhappy* but it brings with it its own *loneliness*. I am *tormented* by my memories and sometimes, I am *assuaged* by them . . . I suffer from a *recurring* dream that I have become a *shadow*" (emphasis added). The emphasized words in the preceding passage suggest the conflict between past and present, youth and old age, the shadowy, ghostly, internal (infernal?) puzzles which haunt all of us. The fact is that the *Passarola* is an invention, a creation which is, in effect, a danger to the rationalism of the Enlightenment. This is especially important because this 'airship' raises important questions. What does it mean to "find oneself between heaven and the abyss?" Is there true ecstasy in the experience of flying? Should the airship, the flying machine, be condemned as an evil thing because it unsettles the common perspective? Should we creatures dare to reach exotic new heights? Thus this deceptive narrative—one that reminds us of Verne, Poe, Stevenson—moves beyond the children's narrative, the juvenile longings we all have to go "beyond the beyond," to see where we begin and end. It is a meta-narrative because the *Passarola* investigates the nature of any creation—including narrative itself. I invoke the name of Leslie Fiedler who explained the 'real' meaning of popular genres, viewing them as secret tales of our unconscious drives. The novel plays with the conflict between stability and instability, vision (dream) and reality. It reminds us that we travel to let "in new colors and feelings." But we also let in demonic frustrations. And where do we finally end? Here or elsewhere? [Irving Malin]

T. C. Boyle. *Tooth and Claw*. Penguin, 2006. 304pp. Paper: $15.00.

T.C. Boyle's seventh collection of stories demonstrates both his mastery and his range, leaving no doubt that he is one of the major fiction writers of our time. *Tooth and Claw* showcases a mature writer at the top of his game. As the title indicates, the neo-naturalist themes of Boyle's recent novel *Drop City* are at play in this collection of fourteen stories. These themes are especially prominent in a few stories: one about a graduate student who joins a pack of dogs, another about a couple stranded in a snowstorm miles from the nearest lodge, another about a disaffected young man who unwillingly becomes the keeper of a feral African cat. The border between human and animal is shadowy in Boyle's fiction, if it exists at all. Many other stories center around the lives of boozy, drug-addled men, set adrift after being rejected by their spouses or lovers, searching for meaning, or attachment, or maybe just the next bar. These characters elicit pathos, but rarely judgment: the reader is more likely to wince than to shake his head in disapproval. Although divorced drunkards dominate the collection, some stories transcend the here and now, such as one that takes place on a remote Scottish island during a severe windstorm, or one that takes place in Argentina as the ozone hole rapidly deteriorates, or even a rewriting of Sarah Kemble Knight's eighteenth-century journey, made famous in her journal. Boyle guides us with a steady hand and a genuine love of language through many fictional worlds. His cynical humor and curiosity about the human condition make this a tremendously entertaining and provocative collection. I didn't want the book to end, but given the author's prolific output in recent years, I probably won't have to wait long for the next one. [D. Quentin Miller]

Christine Montalbetti. *Western.* Paris: POL, 2005. 212pp. €17.50.

Western is Christine Montalbetti's fourth book for the Editions POL, following *Sa fable achevée, Simon sort dans la bruine* [His tale concluded, Simon walks into the drizzle] (2001), *L'Origine de l'homme* [The origin of man] (2002), and *Expérience de la campagne* [Experience of the countryside] (2005). It is a curious novel and a challenging one, principally because events are so scarce. That is all the more disconcerting, since the narrative model that Montalbetti has chosen to work with is that of the Hollywood Western, a genre that invests so heavily in action. Here, however, action is reduced to a bare minimum: characters do amble down the main street of this cowboy town; a stagecoach does arrive; and, two hundred pages into the text, there is finally a gunfight. But that's about it. There is thus very little story here; yet discourse is found in abundance. Indeed, the text is saturated with it, as if Montalbetti wished to test the limits—and exhaust the possibilities—of novelistic discursivity.

Montalbetti draws her focus closer and closer upon what few events she proposes, suggesting narrative inferences and hypotheses that compete for her reader's attention and vex each other in intriguing ways. She solicits her reader's attention constantly and directly, sometimes speaking in her narratorial persona, sometimes in her authorial one. She lays traps and false inferential paths for her reader, at the same time warning her reader to beware of just such ploys. There are moments of what narratologists call "disnarration" here, moments when the text refuses to tell us what happens; and Montalbetti exploits that technique lustily, asking her reader along the way to entertain questions that can have no answer. The flashbacks and flash-forwards that she offers seem to beg the question of narrative organization, in a text with no firmly fixed center. Yet that is undoubtedly one of the points that Montalbetti is making here. For, rather than a tale of cowboys and their adventures, *Western* is in fact a story of writing and reading, and about how stories are constructed and come to *be* in both of those dynamics, through a process that involves both wandering and wondering in equal measure. This is, in short, an obsessional novel—and thus it is well suited to please those individuals who might admit to being obsessive readers of novels. [Warren Motte]

R. M. Berry. *Frank*. Chiasmus Press, 2006. 202pp. Paper: $12.00.

In a world of celebrity novels with perfect skin, hair, and teeth, *Frank* is a monster of letters. Called an "unwriting" of Mary Shelley's *Frankenstein*, R. M. Berry's *Frank* is faithful to its mother's plot: a young man fired by a dream to create goes off to college to immerse himself in his field, allows unbridled enthusiasm to carry him beyond the bounds of all that is held sacred, then spends the rest of his life trying to disavow his creation, first running from it, then trying to destroy it. The unwriting of Shelley's story comes from the fact that in Berry's novel, Frank Stein, the main character and cousin of Gertrude Stein, goes to Harvard to study "American letters"; seeing deeper into the inner workings of his chosen field than his classmates, he ends up creating an experimental novel. Recognizing belatedly what a career-ending first step this can be in a world that holds the novel to be a form of glossy entertainment, he first tries to disavow his creation, then ends up pursuing it into the swamps of language, located in the Florida Everglades, exposing along the way the inherent racism, suppressed sexuality, class bias, and constructed nature of Shelley's foundational story—and many of our own. As with parody, to get the full impact of Berry's unwriting, especially its humor—and this is a *very* funny book—it helps to have Shelley's tale in mind. For example, when Frank tells one of his Harvard professors that he's been reading Heidegger (he of "Origins"), his professor reacts with the same disbelief Victor faces when he tells a biology professor that he'd been reading Galen: "Have you really wasted your precious youth on such nonsense?" As the novel progresses, Frank (and the reader) comes to see that language can be neither taken apart nor manipulated without consequences, that authors—i.e., all of us—bring worlds and real-world consequences into existence through words, be they the things we say to one another, the policies that take a nation to war, or the rewriting of the genetic code that will bring a new form of cultural and biological life into existence. Given the current state of the state and of literature, it's hard to imagine a novel directed more at the heart of America than is Berry's *Frank*, a philosophical tour de force that demonstrates what the novel still does better than any other medium. [Steve Tomasula]

Valerie Martin. *The Unfinished Novel*. Vintage, 2006. 224pp. Paper: $13.00.

Although I reviewed *The Great Divorce*, I want to mention Martin's best-known novel, *Mary Reilly*. That book was made into a move starring Julia Roberts, who is the servant of the strange Dr. Jekyll. Her point of view gives us a wonderful perception of her master—she can't understand his odd behavior. The novel explores gender, and perverse desire, in a startling way. In this brilliant collection of stories, all relationships are edgy, questionable, oblique; they tend to unsettle us. In "The Change," the title could refer to aging or the movement of lust to the acceptance of "everyday love." Evan wonders whether his Gina has left him. The imagery of the last page is overwhelming. He sees in an "uncanny way" that he is being watched by an owl: "He could see the talons sticking out beneath the thick brown fluff of the legs, black and long and sharp as a cats' claws." Evan's vision is so momentous that he forgets about Gina: "With the intrusion of this portentious creature, all the tedium and anxiety of his life had fallen away." In the title story, the narrator returns to New Orleans and he meets Rita, whom he had not seen for twenty years. She has changes into an "overweight woman, not a sight to provoke my interest." Rita claims to have been writing a huge novel; she eventually leaves it in his care, hoping that as a well-known author, he will find a publisher. He thinks: "If Rita's book was published my part in that process would be part of the packaging." The narrator likens his position to that of Max Brod, who was told by Kafka to destroy his life's art. The reference to Kafka not only alerts us to the relation of Martin to the author who, perhaps, is our greatest writer—it offers a parallel to her own simple but frightening talent. Does the narrator publish the manuscript or does he bury it? Does he feel any obligation to his old relationship with Rita? Such questions are answered ambiguously, although the last words give us a hint. The six stories in the collection are fascinating portraits of driven artists who try to deal with "reality." They explore subtly what James called the "madness of art." Or to quote from Martin's "Beethoven:" "And the real world has got to be a lot more comfortable than the one I'm living in." Which is what, would you say, some kind of anti-reality? A counter-world? [Irving Malin]

Stacey Levine. *Frances Johnson*. Clear Cut Press, 2005. 230pp. Paper: $12.95.

The gift of Stacey Levine's fiction lies in making mundane life strange in order to reveal the normally invisible forces that shape us—in all their absurd permutations. Similar to *Dra—* , Levine's previous novel in which the title character's search for a job is also a search for identity, the Frances of *Frances Johnson* is forced to decide whether or not to attend the Munson town dance. In other words, Frances faces an existential crisis: going to the dance as all the people of Munson pressure her to do equates with becoming part of "normal" society while not attending, or even more astonishing, leaving town for neighboring Little Munson, is an admission that she'll always be alone, different, ostracized. As the names of these sister cities indicate, no matter where you go, there you are. Though Frances knows that she can't be who she isn't, she can't figure out who she is either. So she meanders from mother to doctor to teacher asking in various ways "if a town can slowly smash a girl by dismantling her personality in dozens of small ways." Each encounter is an opportunity for misunderstanding, shame, humiliation or anger. When Frances questions the dry crackers everyone in Munson lives off of, her sister faults her attitude, not the town's inertia, yelling at Frances to "be creative—mash them up with corn. . . ." Her desire to work with animals is understood as a desire to work in a slaughterhouse. Whatever is "wrong" with Frances is invisible to her and the rest of Munson because it has no name. Told through deadpan humor and lean prose, the soul searching and histrionics of *Frances Johnson* come across as a mash-up between girl's coming-of-age genre fiction and Beckett: an existential journey that is as hilarious as it is profound. [Steve Tomasula]

Jonathan Coe. *The Closed Circle*. Vintage, 2006. 367pp. Paper: $14.00.

The Closed Circle continues, and to some degree completes, Jonathan Coe's 2001 novel *The Rotters' Club*. While that narrative was set in a Birmingham, England of the mid-to late-1970s, during the major characters' adolescence, this one moves things ahead 25 years to the late 1990s and the early years of the current decade. In form, *The Closed Circle* is a mirror image of the earlier book. *The Rotters' Club* consisted of three sections of 10, 28, and 1 chapters, respectively, and the new novel's three sections have 1, 28, and 10 chapters—numbered in reverse. The circle, in other words, is closed. Circles abound in the novel: close circles of friends, closed circles of political intrigue, closed circles of historical repetition. The mysteries of *The Rotters' Club* are cleared up here, some in surprising ways. The racism and IRA terrorism that were central to the first novel's plot are still important, and Coe adds more recent historical developments—industrial plant closures, the migration of Tony Blair's "New Labour" to the political center, September 11, the war on Iraq. Through it all his now-older characters struggle to find purpose in lives that, in many cases, haven't fulfilled their early promise. Even though one of them says, "We've all ended up with what we wanted . . . We've all lived happily ever after," happiness here comes highly qualified. The book is rich with Coe's characteristic humor, and with a slow-burning anger as well, anger at the ways in which individuals, communities, and nations are manipulated for corporate and political gain. Though it includes a synopsis of *The Rotters' Club*, *The Closed Circle* will mean the most to those who have already read the first novel. Taken together these two books comprise a remarkable alternate history of the last thirty years. [Stephen Bernstein]

Books Received

Adichie, Chimamanda Ngozi. *Half of a Yellow Sun,* Alfred A. Knopf, $24.95. (F)

Addonizio, Kim. *Little Beauties*, Simon & Schuster, 2006. $13.00. (F)

Amdahl, Gary. *Visigoth*, Milkweed Editions, 2006. $15.95. (F)

Bailey, Peter J. *Rabbit (Un) Redeemed: The Drama of Belief in John Updike's Fiction*, Farleigh Dickinson University Press, 2006. $52.50. (NF)

Behrens, Peter. *The Law of Dreams*, Steerforth Press, 2006. $24.95. (F)

Bonucci, Silvia. *Voices from a Time*, Steerforth Press, 2006. $12.95. (F)

Cheek, Angie, and Lacy Hunter Nix, eds. *The Foxfire 40th Anniversary Book*, Anchor Books, 2006. $17.95. (NF)

DeShell, Jeffrey. *Peter*, Starcherone Books, 2006. $18.00. (F)

Dibdin, Michael. *Back to Bologna*, Vintage, 2006. $12.95. (F)

Edwards, Sonia. *White Tree*, Dufour Editions, 2006. $14.95. (F)

Feast, Jim, and Ron Kolm. *Neo Phobe*, Unbearable Books, 2006. $12.00. (F)

Forrester, Gary. *Houseboating in the Ozarks*, Dufour Editions, 2006. $24.95. (F)

Giles, James R. *The Spaces of Violence*, The University of Alabama Press, 2006. $42.50. (NF)

Grandbois, Peter. *The Gravedigger*, Chronicle Books, 2006. $23.95. (F)

Grant, Richard. *Another Green World*, Alfred A. Knopf, 2006. $24.95. (F)

Gregory, Philippa. *Virgin Earth*, Touchstone, 2006. $16.00. (F)

Hodgen, Christine. *Hello, I Must Be Going*, W.W. Norton & Company, 2006. $23.95. (F)

Khadra, Yasmina. *The Attack*, Nan A. Talese/Doubleday, 2006. $24.95. (F)

Kohler, Sheila. *Children of Pithiviers*, Other Press, 2006. $13.95. (F)

—. *Cracks*, Other Press, 2006. $13.95. (F)

Joern, Pamela Carter. *The Floor of the Sky*, University of Nebraska Press, 2006. $16.95. (F)

Joss, Morag. *Puccini's Ghost*, Delacorte Press, 2006. $22.00. (F)

Mathisen, Robert R., ed. *Critical Issues in American Religious History*, Baylor University Press, 2006. $44.95. (NF)

Meckler, Michael, ed., *Classical Antiquity and the Politics of America*, Baylor University Press, 2006. $29.95. (NF)

McLean, Beresford. *Providence Pond*, Anancy Books, 2006. $17.95. (F)

Oderman, Kevin. *Going*, Vandalia Press, 2006. $16.50. (F)

Olson, Kirby. *Temping*, Black Heron, 2005. $22.95. (F)

Parai, Kalobaran. *A Father's SMS*, Kamala Press, 2006. $10.00. (P)

Perabo, Susan. *Who I Was Supposed to Be*, Simon & Schuster, 2006. $14.00. (F)

Reifler, Nelly. *See Through*, Simon & Schuster, 2006. $13.00. (F)

Robbins, Tom. *Wild Ducks Flying Backward*, Bantam, 2006. $12.00. (F)

Sancton, Tom. *Song for My Fathers*, Other Press, 2006. $24.95. (NF)

Shukman, Henry. *Mortimer of the Maghreb*, Alfred A. Knopf, 2006. $24.00. (F)

Smith, R. Drew, ed., *Freedom's Distant Shores: American Protestants and Post-Colonial Alliances with Africa*, Baylor University Press, 2006. $29.95. (NF)

Spencer, Nicholas. *After Utopia: The Rise of Critical Space in Twentieth-Century American Fiction*, University of Nebraska Press, 2006. $39.95. (NF)

Steinberg, Susan. *Hydroplane*, FC2, 2006. $15.95. (F)

van der Jagt, Marek. *The Story of My Baldness*, Other Press, 2006. $13.95. (F)

Vivian, Robert. *The Mover of Bones,* University of Nebraska Press, 2006. $23.95. (F)

Winthrop, Elizabeth Hartley. *Fireworks*, Alfred A. Knopf, 2006. $23.95. (F)

Contributors

Writers

ALEJANDRO AGUILAR (Camagüey, 1958), although trained as a historian, has worked mainly in the performing arts, as a lecturer at U.S. universities, and as a training developer in the software industry. He is the author of three novels *La desobediencia* [Disobedience]; *Casa de cambio* [Bureau of exchange]—which merited an honorable mention for the 1997 Italo Calvino Prize and was published both in Puerto Rico and mainland U.S.; and *Razones para llamar a Sandra*—which was a finalist in the 2001 Casa de las Américas Prize for Fiction; and two collections of short stories: *Paisaje de arcilla* [Clay landscape] and *Figuras tendidas* [Stretched out figures], which won the Manuel Cofiño Prize in 1999.

AIDA BAHR (Havana, 1958) has recently completed a novel, *Las voces y los ecos* [Voices and echoes], and is at work on another one. She is director of a publishing house in Santiago, Cuba, Ediciones Oriente, and editor of their magazine. Her work has appeared in many anthologies in Spanish and in translation. She is the author of several collections of stories, including *Hay un gato en la ventana* [There's a cat in the window] (1984), *Ellas de noche* [Women at night] (1989), *Espejísmos* [Mirror images] (1998), and several screenplays.

JESÚS DAVID CURBELO (Camagüey, 1965) has published many volumes of poetry and several short story collections, including *Cuentos para adúlteros* [Stories for adulterers] (1995) and *Tres tristes triángulos* [Three sad triangles] (2000), and two novels: *Inferno* in 1999 and *Diario de un poeta recién cazado* [Diary of a newly caught poet] (1999). The many prizes he has won include the David Prize for Poetry in 1991 and the José Soler Puig Award for fiction in 1998.

EDUARDO DEL LLANO (Moscow, 1962) has lived in Havana since 1964, and has a degree in Art History from the University of Havana. A writer of fiction, poetry, essays and film scripts, he has published collections of poetry (*Nostalgia de la babosa*, 1993), six novels (some in collaboration with others), the most recent of which are *La clessidra di Nicanor* (1997), *Obstáculo* (1997) and *Tres* (2002). His eight collections of short stories include *Criminales* (1994), *El beso y el plan* (1997), *Cabeza de ratón* (1998) and *Los viajes de Nicanor* (2000). He has taught Latin American art, photography and film studies at the University of Havana and elsewhere, has won many prizes and awards, and has participated in many international film festivals.

ADELAIDA FERNÁNDEZ DE JUAN (Havana, 1961) is a physician specializing in internal medicine, and author of many short stories, including those published in the volumes *Dolly y otros cuentos africanos* (1994) about her experiences in Zambia between 1988 and 1990. It appeared in English as *Dolly and Other African Tales*. Her second story collection, *Oh vida* [Oh life] (1998) won the National Short Story Prize of the Cuban National Union of Writers and Artists. Her story "El beso" [The kiss] received Honorable Mention in the 2004 Julio Cortázar Short Story Competition. *La hija de Darío* [Darió's daughter], her third book of stories, won the 2004 Alejo Carpentier Prize. *Nadie es profeta* [No one is a prophet], her first novel, was published in 2006.

FRANCISCO GARCÍA GONZÁLEZ (Havana, 1963) has a degree in History from Havana University. He is a writer, editor, and screenwriter. His short story collections include *Juegos permitidos* [Games allowed] (1994), *Color local* [Local color] (1999) and *¿Qué quieren las mujeres?* [What do women want?] (2003). He has also published a historical essay, *Presidio Modelo, temas escondidos* [Model prison, hidden agendas] (2002), and *Historia sexual de la nación* (2006). His stories have appeared in anthologies in Cuba, Spain, and the U.S. He won Cuba's Hemingway Short Story Prize in 1999, and has served as editor of the cultural journal *Habáname*. His articles have appeared in periodicals in Cuba, Mexico, Chile and the U.S. He is the author of many film scripts.

ALEXIS SEBASTIÁN GARCÍA SOMODEVILLA (Havana, 1964) won the Caimán Barbudo prize in 1989, for his collection of short stories, *El deshollinador* [The chimney sweep], published in Cienfuegos in 2000. His collection *Senderos virtuales* [Virtual paths] was published in 2002. He is the Librarian of the Archivo Provincial Histórico of Cienfuegos.

RONALDO MENÉNDEZ PLASENCIA was born in Havana, Cuba in 1970. His stories have appeared in numerous anthologies in Cuba including *Los últimos serán los primeros*; *Anuario de la UNEAC 1994*; *Fábula de ángeles*; and *El ánfora del diablo*, among others. He is the author of four books: *Alguien se va lamiendo todo* (Premio David, Ediciones Union, 1996); *El derecho al pataleo de los ahorcados* (Premio Casa de las Américas, Lengua de Trapo, 1998); *La piel de Inessa*,

(Premio Lengua de trapo de Narrativa, Spain, 1999); and *De modo que esto es la muerte* (Cuento, Lengua de Trapo, Madrid, 2002).

MIGUEL MEJIDES (Camagüey, 1950) won the David prize for his 1977 book *Tiempo de hombres* (Time of men), the 1981 UNEAC Rodríguez prize for *El jardín de las flores silvestres* (The wildflower garden) and the Juan Rulfo short story prize in 1994 for "Rumba-Palace," published in 1996. He has also published novels such as *La habitación terrestre* (Inhabiting the Earth) and *Perversiones en el Prado* (Perversions in the Prado).

LEONARDO PADURA FUENTES (Havana, 1955) essayist, journalist, and novelist is famous for his series of detective novels ("The Four Seasons") featuring the exploits of Mario Conde. He has received numerous national and international prizes and has published two books of stories: *Según los años pasan* [As the years go by] and *La puerta de Alcalá y otras cacerías* [The Alcalá Gate and other hunting scenes]. He has published books of interviews about salsa and baseball, as well as many critical essays. Recent works include: *Adiós Hemingway* [Goodbye Hemingway] (2001), *Culture and the Cuban Revolution* with John Kirk in 2001, and another Mario Conde novel, *La neblina del ayer* [The mist of yesterday] (2005). His works have been translated into numerous languages.

ANTONIO JOSÉ PONTE is a poet, fiction writer and essayist. Two collections of his poems have been published: *Poesía (1982-1989)* (Ediciones Letras Cubanas, 1991) and *Asiento en las ruinas* (Ediciones Letras Cubanas, 1997). He has published five collections of essays. Two volumes of his short stories have been published in English translation: *In the Cold of the Malecón*, translated by Cola Franzen and Dick Cluster (City Lights, 2002) and *Tales From the Cuban Empire*, translated by Cola Franzen (City Lights, 2002). His first novel, *Contrabando de sombras* [Trafficking in shadows], was published by Monadori (Barcelona, 2002). He recently completed a second novel titled *La fiesta vigilada* [The closely watched fiesta], to be published in Spain by Anagrama in 2007. He lives in Havana.

ENA LUCÍA PORTELA, (Havana, 1972) is a novelist and short story writer. She won the UNEAC National Novel Prize in 1997 for her first novel *El pájaro: tinta china y pincel* [The bird: Chinese ink and pen], which was published in 1999 along with her collection of short stories, *Una extraña entre las piedras* [A strange woman among the stones]. She was the recipient of the Juan Rulfo Short Story Prize given by Radio France International in 1999 for her short story, "El viejo, el asesino y yo" ["The old man, the assassin and I"]. Her novel

La sombra del caminante [The walker's shadow] was published in 2001, and a third novel, *Cien botellas en una pared* [One hundred bottles on a wall], won the Jaén Novel Prize in Spain in 2002.

JOSÉ ANTONIO QUINTANA VEIGA lives in Nueva Gerona on Cuba's Isle of Youth. He has published three books of short stories including *Precio de los zapatos* [The price of shoes] (Nueva Gerona, 2002) and the novel *Callejera*. His story "Mi amor y mi caña," ["My love and my sugarcane"] included here, won the first honorable mention in the annual best short story contest of *La Gaceta de Cuba*, the magazine of the National Union of Cuban Writers and Artists.

ANNA LIDIA VEGA SEROVA was born in 1968 in St. Petersburg, Russia, to a Cuban father and a Russian mother. She has lived in Havana since she was 20, and writes exclusively in Spanish. She is also a painter. She won the 1996 Special Prize of the Asociación Hermanos Saíz, and the 1997 Premio David for her collection of stories *Bad Painting* (1997). Her second volume of stories, *Catálogo de mascotas* [Catalog of mascots] was published in 1998, and the third, *Limpiando ventanas y espejos* [Cleaning windows and mirrors] in 2001. Her most recent book is a novel, *Noche de ronda* [Nightwatch] (2004).

MIRTA YÁÑEZ (Havana, 1947), has written fiction, poetry, literary criticism, and children's books, and has taught Latin American literature at the University of Havana. In 1988 and 1990 she won the Critics' Prize for the story collection *El Diablo son las cosas* [To the devil with it] and for the essay *La narrativa del romanticismo en Latinoamérica* [Romantic narrative in Latin America]. Other books she has published include *Las visitas y otros poemas* [The visits and other poems] (1986) and *Una memoria de elefante* [An elephant's memory] (1991). She is the co-editor of the anthology of Cuban women's stories *Estatuas de sal* [Pillars of salt] (1996), and the editor of *Cubana: Contemporary Fiction by Cuban Women* (1998).

Translators

MARY G. BERG's recent translations from Spanish include collections, *Open Your Eyes and Soar: Cuban Women Writing Now* (2003); novels, *I've Forgotten Your Name* (2004) by Martha Rivera (Dominican Republic), *River of Sorrows* (2000) by Libertad Demitrópulos (Argentina), and *Ximena at the Crossroads* (1998) by Laura Riesco (Peru); and stories, women's travel accounts, literary criticism, and collections of poetry, most recently *Quincunx* and *The Book of Giulio Camillo* by Carlota Caulfield (Cuba) and *Antonio Machado's*

The Landscape of Castile (with Dennis Maloney). She teaches at Harvard Extension and is a Resident Scholar at the Women's Studies Research Center at Brandeis University, where she writes about Latin American writers, including Clorinda Matto de Turner, Juana Manuela Gorriti, Soledad Acosta de Samper, and contemporary Cubans.

PAMELA CARMELL teaches Spanish in St. Louis. She has translated Luisa Valenzuela, Manuel Puig, Gloria Fuertes, and Delmira Agustini, among others. Her translations have appeared in numerous journals and anthologies. Her translation of Antonio Larreta's novel, *The Last Portrait of the Duchess of Alba*, was a Book of the Month Club selection. Her translation of poems by Belkis Cuza Male, *Woman on the Front Lines*, received the Witter Bynner Prize. She is co-translator of *With Eyes and Soul*, poems by Nancy Morejón, published by White Pine Press in 2004.

DICK CLUSTER's translations of Cuban fiction include *Cubana: Contemporary Ficton by Cuban Women* (Beacon, 1998, ed. Mirta Yáñez, tr. with Cindy Schuster); Pedro de Jesús's *Frigid Tales* (City Lights, 2002); Alejandro Hernández Diaz's *The Cuban Mile* (Latin American Literary Review Press, 1998); Antonio José Ponte's *In the Cold of the Malecón and Other Stories* (City Lights, 2000); Leonardo Padura's *Mascaras* (selection, Whereabouts Press, 2002); and Abel Prieto's *The Flight of the Cat* (Random House Mondadori, forthcoming). He is also the author of the novels *Return to Sender* (Dutton, 1988), *Repulse Monkey* (Dutton, 1989), and *Obligtions of the Bone* (St. Martins, 1992), and translator of Cuban political scientist Rafael Hernández's essay collection *Looking at Cuba* (University Press of Florida, 2003).

CRISTINA DE LA TORRE has translated novels by Rosa Montero (Spain), Carmen Riera (Spain) and Nora Strejilevich (Argentina), as well as numerous short stories, many of them by authors from Cuba—where she was born. She has received translation fellowships from NEH, the Howard Foundation, and the Banff International Centre for Translation. De la Torre lives in Atlanta and teaches Spanish and literary translation at Emory University.

ANNE (ANITA) FOUNTAIN was born in Buenos Aires and earned graduate degrees at Indiana University and Columbia University. She teaches Latin American literature and culture, and coordinates Latin American Studies at San José State University. Her recent publications include: *José Martí and U.S. Writers* (2003) and *Versos Sencillos: A Dual Language Edition* (2005). Her translations of

Martí's poetry have also appeared in: *The New Anthology of American Poetry (Vol. I: Traditions and Revolutions, Beginnings to 1900)* (2003); *A History of Modern Latin America* (2nd edition) (2005); and *Bomb Magazine*, summer 2004. Her translation of Nancy Alonso's *Cerrado por reparación* [Closed for Repairs] is forthcoming from Curbstone Press.

COLA FRANZEN's recent publications include a bilingual edition of *Horses in the Air and Other Poems* by Jorge Guillén (City Lights, 1999), which won the Harold Morton Landon Translation Prize awarded by the Academy of American Poets; *All Night Movie*, a novel by Alicia Borinsky, translated with the author (Northwestern University Press, 2002), and two volumes of work by Saúl Yurkievich: a collection of poems, *Background Noise/ Ruido de fondo*, and a collection of prose pieces, *In the Image and Likeness* (Catbird Press, 2003). In 2004 she received the Gregory Kolovakis Award from PEN American Center. She lives in Cambridge, Massachusetts.

LOUISE POPKIN's translations of Latin American poetry, drama and fiction have appeared in literary journals such as *Beacons, Kenyon Review, Triquarterly* and *Mid-American Review* and in anthologies of literature in translation. Authors whose work she has translated include Claribel Alegría (Nicaragua); Ricardo Elizondo and Héctor Manjarrez (Mexico); Margarita Niemayer and Sonia González Valdenegro (Chile); and Mempo Giardinelli and Juan Gelman (Argentina), Mario Benedetti, Teresa Porzcekanski, Leo Masliah, Idea Vilariño, Amanda Berenguer, Eduardo Galeano, Hugo Achugar, Hiber Conteris and Mauricio Rosencof (Uruguay). Her most recent publication is a translation of Rosencof's *The Letters that Never Came* (University of New Mexico Press, 2004). She divides her time between Montevideo, Uruguay, and the Boston area, where she teaches Spanish at Harvard Extension.

Guatemalan-born DAVID UNGER has just completed a new novel called *In My Eyes, You Are Beautiful*. He is the author of *Life in the Damn Tropics* (Syracuse University Press, 2002, University of Wisconsin Press, 2004, [*Vivir en el maldito trópico*, Random House Mondadori, Mexico, 2004; Recorded Books 2005; Locus Publishing, Taiwan, 2006 and Yingpan Brother Publishing, China, 2007]). He has translated eleven books, among them Teresa Cárdenas's *Letters to My Mother* (Groundwood Books, 2006); Rigoberta Menchú's *The Honey Jar* (Groundwood Books, 2006) and *The Girl from Chimel* (Groundwood Books, 2005); Ana María Machado's *Me in the Middle* (Groundwood Press, 2002); Silvia Molina's *The Love You Promised Me* (Curbstone Press, 1999)—which won the Sor Juana Inés de la

Cruz Prize and was short-listed for the 2001 IMPAC Prize; *The Popol Vuh* (Groundwood Press, 1999); Elena Garro's *First Love* (Curbstone Press); Bárbara Jacobs *The Dead Leaves* (Curbstone Press); and Nicanor Parra's *Antipoems: New and Selected* (New Directions).

Annual Index

References are to issue number and pages, respectively

Contributors

Books Reviewed

Reviewers' names follow in parentheses. Regular reviewers are abbreviated: JB=Jeff Bursey; JMD=Jeremy M. Davies; IM=Irving Malin; WM=Warren Motte; MP=Michael Pinker.

CONJUNCTIONS:47

Twenty-fifth Anniversary Issue

This special Twenty-fifth Anniversary Issue celebrates a quarter century of innovative contemporary writing and features new work by some of the most distinguished voices of the day.

The issue presents new fiction, poetry, and essays by Jim Crace, Richard Powers, Lydia Davis, Jonathan Lethem, William H. Gass, Robert Coover, Joyce Carol Oates, Russell Banks, John Ashbery, Ann Lauterbach, John Barth, Rikki Ducornet, William T. Vollmann, Barbara Guest, Mary Caponegro, C. D. Wright, Peter Straub, Edie Meidav, Howard Norman, Forrest Gander, Jorie Graham, Rick Moody, Christopher Sorrentino, Maureen Howard, Jonathan Carroll, Shelley Jackson, Scott Geiger, Ben Marcus, Robert Antoni, Diane Williams, Lyn Hejinian, Rae Armantrout, Micheline Aharonian Marcom, and many others.

Conjunctions:47, Twenty-fifth Anniversary Issue, is a must-read for anyone interested in contemporary letters.

CONJUNCTIONS
Edited by Bradford Morrow
Published by Bard College
Annandale-on-Hudson, NY 12504

To order, phone 845-758-1539
or visit www.conjunctions.com
$15.00

DELILLO FIEDLER GASS PYNCHON
University of Delaware Press
Collections on Contemporary Masters

UNDERWORDS
Perspectives on Don DeLillo's *Underworld*

Edited by Joseph Dewey, Steven G. Kellman, and Irving Malin

Essays by Jackson R. Bryer, David Cowart, Kathleen Fitzpatrick, Joanne Gass, Paul Gleason, Donald J. Greiner, Robert McMinn, Thomas Myers, Ira Nadel, Carl Ostrowski, Timothy L. Parrish, Marc Singer, and David Yetter

$39.50

INTO *THE TUNNEL*
Readings of Gass's Novel

Edited by Steven G. Kellman and Irving Malin

Essays by Rebecca Goldstein, Donald J. Greiner, Brooke Horvath, Marcus Klein, Jerome Klinkowitz, Paul Maliszewski, James McCourt, Arthur Saltzman, Susan Stewart, and Heide Ziegler

$35.00

LESLIE FIEDLER AND AMERICAN CULTURE

Edited by Steven G. Kellman and Irving Malin

Essays by John Barth, Robert Boyers, James M. Cox, Joseph Dewey, R.H.W. Dillard, Geoffrey Green, Irving Feldman, Leslie Fiedler, Susan Gubar, Jay L. Halio, Brooke Horvath, David Ketterer, R.W.B. Lewis, Sanford Pinsker, Harold Schechter, Daniel Schwarz, David R. Slavitt, Daniel Walden, and Mark Royden Winchell

$36.50

PYNCHON AND *MASON & DIXON*

Edited by Brooke Horvath and Irving Malin

Essays by Jeff Baker, Joseph Dewey, Bernard Duyfhuizen, David Foreman, Donald J. Greiner, Brian McHale, Clifford S. Mead, Arthur Saltzman, Thomas H. Schaub, David Seed, and Victor Strandberg

$39.50

ORDER FROM ASSOCIATED UNIVERSITY PRESSES
2010 Eastpark Blvd., Cranbury, New Jersey 08512
PH 609-655-4770   FAX 609-655-8366   E-mail AUP440@ aol.com

Studies *in* American Fiction

A journal of articles and reviews on the prose fiction of the United States

Published semiannually by the Department of English, Northeastern University

Mary Loeffelholz, Editor

Recent numbers include

Annual subscriptions: $12.00 for individuals, $15.00 for individuals outside the United States; $18.00 for domestic institutions, $20.00 for institutions outside the United States. Send subscriptions and inquiries to Studies in American Fiction, Department of English, 406 Holmes Hall, Northeastern University, Boston MA 02115-5000. Phone: 617-373-3687; fax: 617-373-2509; e-mail: americanfiction@neu.edu

NOON

NOON

A LITERARY ANNUAL

1369 MADISON AVENUE   PMB 298
NEW YORK   NEW YORK   10128-0711

EDITION PRICE $9 DOMESTIC $14 FOREIGN

Dalkey Archive
Scholarly Series

Order any of the following Scholarly Series titles from
WWW.DALKEYARCHIVE.COM before January 1, 2007,
and receive 25% off the cover price

Don't Ever Get Famous:
Essays on New York Writing after the New York School
ED. BY DANIEL KANE

The Walk:
Notes on a Romantic Image
JEFFREY C. ROBINSON

Mindscreen:
Bergman, Godard, and First-Person Film
BRUCE F. KAWIN

The Mind of the Novel:
Reflexive Fiction and the Ineffable
BRUCE F. KAWIN

These essays focus attention on the vibrant downtown New York poetry scene of the 1960s and '70s. Contributors examine the cultural, sociological, and historical contexts of a diverse and important group of writers, including Bernadette Mayer, Lorenzo Thomas, Hannah Weiner, Clark Coolidge, Anne Waldman, and many others. The poetry coming out of the downtown scene proved crucial for American innovative writing as a whole, and this volume is a vital and groundbreaking book that finally begins to address a major gap in literary history and criticism.

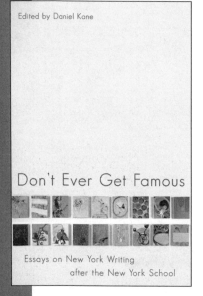

Don't Ever Get Famous:
Essays on New York Writing
after the New York School

ED. BY DANIEL KANE

Dalkey Archive Scholarly Series
Literary Criticism
$34.95 / paper
ISBN-13: 978-1-56478-460-5
ISBN-10: 1-56478-460-6

"Not concerned with 'creating a literary mafia or codifying a poetics,' as Anne Waldman has put it, New York's downtown poets of the '60s and '70s largely await discovery. This collection of essays does a fine job of showing how varied and complex their achievements were. It might just get them famous after all."
—Peter Nicholls

"By collecting these superb essays by poets and critics, Daniel Kane has taken the door off its hinges and let the wind from the East River blow afresh through the house of poetry."
—Michael Davidson

The Walk, a meditation on walking and on the literature of walking, ruminates on this pervasive, even commonplace, modern image. It is not so much an argument as a journey along the path of literature, noting the occasions and settings, the pleasures and possibilities of different types of walking, and the many literatures walking has produced. Jeffrey C. Robinson's discussion is less criticism than appreciation. With an autobiographical bent, he leads the reader through Romantic, modern, and contemporary literature to show us the shared pleasures of reading, writing, and walking.

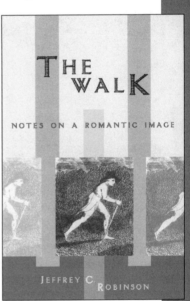

The Walk:
Notes on a Romantic Image

JEFFREY C. ROBINSON
AFTERWORD BY ROGER GILBERT

Dalkey Archive Scholarly Series
Literary Criticism
$19.95 / paper
ISBN-13: 978-1-56478-459-9
ISBN-10: 1-56478-459-2

"Jeffrey C. Robinson's *The Walk* is a lively and intelligent omnibus for thinkers as well as for walkers. His evident love of literature is a genuine enthusiasm for all that is best in life."
—Annie Dillard

"The Walk is a stunning, revealing, and thought-provoking revision of Romantic studies, one that forces us to reexamine the conditions of our own lives and minds."
—*Wordsworth Circle*

The first book-length study of reflexivity in the cinema, this groundbreaking work examines the relationship between first-person and self-conscious narration, anchoring its contributions to narrative theory in rich, close readings of films that range from *Sherlock Jr.*, *Citizen Kane*, and a Bugs Bunny cartoon to *Persona* and *2 or 3 Things I Know about Her*. Ultimately, Kawin shows how the reflexivity of film stimulates the aesthetic, political, and psychological processes of the audience, making possible a greater knowledge and acceptance of ourselves.

Mindscreen:
Bergman, Godard, and First-Person Film

Bruce F. Kawin

Dalkey Archive Scholarly Series
Film Criticism
$24.95 / paper
ISBN-13: 978-1-56478-461-2
ISBN-10: 1-56478-461-4

"One of the most thought-provoking film books of recent years."

—*Film Quarterly*

"Bruce Kawin has tackled a subject increasingly crucial to our understanding of cinema history, theory, and practice, and, when all is said and done, his very good book is the one that got there first.... It is richly worth taking up."

—*Film Comment*

From *Moby-Dick* to *The Unnamable*, from *A Tale of a Tub* to *The Book of Questions*, Bruce Kawin passionately explores the nature of self-conscious fiction and compares its structure to that of human consciousness. Many first-person texts—including those of Melville, Stein, Proust, Faulkner, Lessing, and Beckett—involve a hierarchy of narrators or a system of displaced viewpoints, underneath which may lie one ideal voice: a "mind of the novel." Contemporary fiction, he shows, is not a "literature of exhaustion" but a confrontation by the author, text, and reader of the limits of awareness.

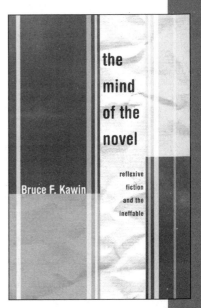

The Mind of the Novel:
Reflexive Fiction and the Ineffable

BRUCE F. KAWIN

Dalkey Archive Scholarly Series
Literary Criticism
$29.95 / paper
ISBN-13: 978-1-56478-462-9
ISBN-10: 1-56478-462-2

"Kawin's analyses are fresh, insightful, informed, and provocative. His erudition is impressive and the 'play' of his mind a source of pleasure and delight. By virtue of its range, nuance, and grace, *The Mind of the Novel* is essential reading for anyone concerned with the ins and outs of reflexive fiction."

—*Contemporary Literature*

"Ambitious, far-ranging. . . . Strongly recommended."

—*Choice*

ORDER FORM

Individuals may use this form to subscribe to the *Review of Contemporary Fiction* or to order back issues of the *Review* and Dalkey Archive titles at a discount (see below for details).

Title	ISBN	Quantity	Price

Subtotal _____

Less Discount _____
(10% for one book, 20% for two or more books)

Subtotal _____

Plus Postage _____
(domestic: $3 + $1 per book / foreign: $5 + $3 per book)

1 Year Individual Subscription to the **Review** _____
($17 domestic, $20.50 foreign)

Total _____

Mailing Address _____

_____

_____

_____

xxvi/3

Credit card payment ☐ Visa ☐ Mastercard

Acct. # _____ Exp. Date _____

Name on card _____ Phone # _____

Please make checks (in U.S. dollars only) payable to *Dalkey Archive Press*

mail or fax this form to: Dalkey Archive Press, ISU Campus Box 8905, Normal, IL 61790-8905; *fax:* 309.438.7422; *tel:* 309.438.7555